Making *it* Happen *in* Sales

3-25-08

Linda
Enjoyed having
You As Neighbors
Henry

Making *it* Happen *in* Sales

HENRY THOMAS

Tate Publishing & *Enterprises*

Making It Happen in Sales

Published by Tate Publishing & Enterprises, LLC
127 E. Trade Center Terrace | Mustang, Oklahoma 73064 USA
1.888.361.9473 | www.tatepublishing.com

Tate Publishing is committed to excellence in the publishing industry. The company reflects the philosophy established by the founders, based on Psalm 68:11, *"The Lord gave the word and great was the company of those who published it."*

Cover design by Elizabeth Mason
Interior design by Stephanie Woloszyn

Published in the United States of America

ISBN: 978-1-60247-928-9
1. Business-Sales
2. Customer Service-Market Place
07.10.31

Dedication & Acknowledgments

This book is dedicated to all of the people that have stopped by to thank me after one of my presentations. It is also dedicated to those who have read my articles and written or e-mailed me with new ideas for articles. Lastly, it is dedicated to you, the new readers, whose first knowledge of me will come through this book.

I have been fortunate in writing this book to have my wonderful brother in-law, Lt. Col. Darryl Freed, USAF retired, as my editor, supporter, and researcher. Most of all, Darryl has been my inspiration.

Table of Contents

Foreword 9

How To Use This Book 11
Overview

Chapter 1. 17
The Basics of Selling

Chapter 2. 25
Create the Desire to Buy

Chapter 3. 39
The Power of Questions

Chapter 4. 51
Learn to Interview Well

Chapter 5. 57
Ways to Deal with Objections

Chapter 6. 69
The Pricing Issue

Chapter 7. 77
Consummating (Closing) the Sale

Chapter 8. 83
Think Like A Winner

Chapter 9. 97
Set and Achieve Your Goals

Chapter 10. 113
Rely on Marketing and Prospecting, Not Hope

Chapter 11 121
What It Takes to Sell in Difficult Times

Chapter 12 135
How to Sell to Women Buyers

Chapter 13 141
Training: How to Guarantee Results

Chapter 14 149
Team Selling: You Never Sell Alone

Chapter 15 153
Follow-Up: The Road to Referrals

Chapter 16 165
Trust: The Essential Element in Sales

Chapter 17 171
Relationships: Follow the Laws

Chapter 18 181
How Customers Buy (Not How You Sell)

Chapter 19 187
The Marketing Plan to Success

Chapter 20 193
So, You've Decided to Be a Sales Manager

About the Author 207

Foreword

The first time I met face-to-face with Henry Thomas, I knew that his ability to teach and train salespeople was second to none. When you are around him, he immediately engages you in a conversation that involves his passion—helping others become more than they ever dreamed they could be. Since our first meeting, I have always suspected that his passion comes from his own experiences and his unique ability to rise above the ordinary sales training models and use the most effective technique I know—experiential learning. Not that I'm any better or more knowledgeable than others at qualifying a person's ability to teach sales, but in Henry's case, it was something he said to me: "Tell me and I will forget, show me and I will remember, involve me and I will understand."

After reading the advance manuscript of this book, I am delighted that Henry has given his readers tangible, down-to earth ways of understanding the salient steps necessary to build a successful sales career.

He tells his readers the "how- to's" of selling a product or service, such as prospecting, qualifying, presenting and closing, but more importantly, he discusses the person you must become to be successful, such as setting goals, listening skills, and the importance of a professional image.

Henry Thomas is short on theory and long on solid sales experience and research. It is my heartfelt recommendation that you not only read this book, but begin living its principles. After you ingest, digest, and make these ideas and principles your own, I have no doubt that you will develop gold medal attitudes about selling that will lead you to achieve the success that you deserve and ultimately ensure that you live a happier, more productive life.

—David E. Wright, President
The Innovators Group, Inc.

How to Use This Book

This book is designed to do one thing: to increase your ability to sell your product or service by showing you how to:

- find prospective customers or clients
- greet and qualify them
- tell your company's "story"
- overcome objections
- close or consummate a sale
- get referrals

It also discusses the five aspects of listening, and points out the difference between a hard sell (that rarely succeeds) and highly professional selling (that gets results). You'll also learn:

- The difference between closing and consummating a sale
- The importance of having a professional image
- The critical need to satisfy customers
- The necessity of setting goals

As you read this book, keep in mind that the practices and contents of each chapter are based on solid sales experience and research, not on theory. You'll learn systems and techniques that you'd be wise to nurture and support. Selling professionally requires that you both modify behavior and alter preconceived ideas. *And this book gives you ways to do both!*

Learning to sell is a lot like learning to ride a bike. You can't ride to your destination by sitting on the sidelines. Similarly, you have to do more than read this book. You have to practice the techniques presented. As you do, keep in mind, that becoming a master salesperson is a process you can't "conquer" overnight. Work through each chapter point by point—as if you're opening a new door to success with everyone that you come in contact. Then refer to this book after every sale as a way to review how you applied these techniques—and praise yourself for doing well.

A sports agent once said, "Free agency is a business; you have to sell an athlete on 30 different teams. That takes work and knowledge of each team to determine their needs. Its hard work, but you get your dues if you know what you're doing."

As you read, you may question the techniques or processes, or believe some are inappropriate. But comments like "This will never work in my area" might simply mean a technique promoted in this book differs from what you're used to. Human nature says if an approach or technique feels uncomfortable, it's easy to declare that "it won't work" and quickly dismiss it. But keep in mind that the information here has been used *successfully* to sell products and services over time and across the nation. Don't hesitate to open new doors for yourself!

Learning is about taking risks—and taking risks can be uncomfortable. Yet, that's the exciting aspect of the whole selling process—that's where the juice is! So get ready to use these ideas to step outside your comfort zone. When you do, you'll open doors to greater achievements and financial success. And this book is designed to do just that.

—Henry A. Thomas

Overview

This is a wonderful time to be working in the profession of selling.

Regardless of economic ups and downs, this era presents more opportunities for achieving a higher standard of living than ever before. And the engine that makes this happen is the profession of selling. As you continue to upgrade your selling skills, your situation will get even better—and people in lots of other professions can't say that.

In the book, The Millionaire Next Door, Thomas J. Stanley and William D. Danko point out that fully 5 percent of self-made millionaires in America are salespeople who have sold for another company, becoming millionaires in a straightforward way.

First, they became superstars at selling; second, they earned an excellent living as a result of their training and selling efforts; and third, they saved and invested a substantial part of their incomes.

You can too, but your first step is to acquire and hone the excellent skills and knowledge required to succeed in this profession.

Start with the chapter "The Basics of Selling," which reviews the fundamentals of selling. Except for two chapters—"Training for Results" and "So, You've Decided to be a Sales Manager"—all other chapters detail fundamentals on prospecting, presenting, consummating (or closing) a sale, plus asking questions and how to listen to the answers.

The "Team Selling" chapter discusses the importance of having your entire staff sell your operation. Your staff includes, among others, your receptionist, those in your service department, and your contractors. Remember, as critical as sales are to an organization, they're only a part of a larger system—one that includes marketing, image, reputation, advertising, service, availability of financing, even curb appeal and displays. In today's economy, and from this time forward, it also includes the quality of the company's website.

The chapter "Set and Achieve Goals" discusses the benefits of goal setting. If you want a particular goal or result in your life, you can have it—but you have to want it, and you have to be clear about what you want.

Closely related to personal goals is the law of cause and effect. It lives at the core of thoughts and attitudes, and it's the basis of becoming a great salesperson. Do you think about being a super star, a great salesperson? Do you really focus on it continually? Is it the thought that consumes most of your time?

To achieve the success that can be readily available to a sales professional, use this book—and adopt unrelenting positive thinking—to lead you where you've always wanted to go. *It's an exciting journey!*

PEOPLE BECOME WHAT THEY THINK.

"You don't need endless time and perfect conditions. Do it now. Do it today. Do it for twenty minutes and watch your heart start beating."

—Barbara Sher

Chapter 1
The Basics of Selling

While both the world and the profession of selling have changed, the basics of what sales professionals need to do have not.

During recent years, a strong economy has brought a plague to many industries—a plague of complacency that affects both sales teams and management. When in the midst of prosperity, it's easy to believe that the good times will never end. But today, as markets shift and erode, it's critical to revisit the basics of selling.

Focus on the Basics

Refocusing on the basics has a two-fold advantage: First, it's a way to get rid of complacency, and second, it prevents that complacency from creeping back into the selling process. When all else is equal, those who have the best sales effort and skills will succeed—usually at the expense of those who don't.

Because each person has a distinctive personality that influences his or her selling style, some flexibility in style should be permitted. The aim, however, is to build on your style strengths, thus stimulating the confidence and freedom to fully explore your potential.

The combination of a hot economy and good results can lead salespeople to believe their approach is just about perfect. But before you settle into a position of complacency, ask yourself these questions:

- Have you been successful even in a weak market?
- Do you practice all the techniques you have learned?
- Do you attempt to meet, greet, and qualify dominant buying motives with as many prospective buyers as you can?
- Do you take opportunities to demonstrate your product or service as often as possible?

- Do you ask closing questions throughout the sales process?
- Did you put your best effort forward with each and every sale?
- Do you continually prospect for new customers?
- Do you always ask your current and previous customers for referrals?

If you answered "No" to at least two of these questions, keep reading!

Even those who have excelled in sales can, and do, lose their competitive edge when they fail to practice all their skills. While the fundamentals of selling aren't complicated, they're not necessarily easy to assimilate during day-to-day interfaces with prospective buyers. Even if you understand the basic principles of selling, you're not automatically assured that they'll be professionally executed.

Successful selling involves definable steps and measurable skills. Selling, for the most part, requires a set of learned skills *honed by consistent practice in face-to-face selling scenarios*. Like selling, closing or completing a sale is also a process. Just like there's no magic bullet to cure disease, there are no magic "closes" nor a formulaic, "101 ways to close." To be effective as a salesperson, it's important to fully understand and follow certain fundamental steps in the closing process.

I believe it's important to subscribe to one particular method and follow it. But no matter which method you use, *you still must follow certain fundamental steps*, as explained here.

Professional ball players don't make it big unless they understand the basics and fundamentals of their sports.

SELLING IS A PROCESS THAT NEEDS TO BE PRACTICED CONTINUALLY.

Fundamental Steps to Master

1. Start with personal preparation.

Where do you stand on these points?

- You can't create desire for something if you don't understand why it's needed.
- You can't deal effectively against your competitors if you don't know how their product compares to yours.
- You can't earn a prospective buyer's trust and confidence unless you have complete knowledge about your service or product.

And you can't expect a prospective buyer to have confidence in the quality of your service/product if your knowledge and presentation don't reflect the same level of quality.

Be sure you're fully prepared in each of these areas: buyers' need and trust, comparative information, product/service knowledge, and ability to present well.

2. Set contact minimums for better prospecting.

   To prospect effectively, decide on a minimum number of potential customers you will contact each week. Ask for references from friends, relatives, and associates to obtain the names of people who may be potential buyers.

3. Perfect your approach and greeting.

   In a retail scenario, be sure to greet each visitor who walks in the door. Even if you're involved with other customers, acknowledge new arrivals with your eyes, hand gestures, and friendly greetings. Always introduce yourself, ask the person's name, and use it soon after hearing it. Seek common interests and establish rapport before beginning your presentation. When meeting a prospect over the phone, introduce yourself warmly, ask his/her name, use it, and establish rapport—all the while with a smile on your face. Your warm smile can actually be perceived through the telephone lines.

4. Qualify and involve your prospective buyer.

   Ask at least one qualifying question at each step of your presentation. Gain as much information as possible in major qualifying areas, including current situation, timing and urgency, and financial situation as well as needs and dominant buying motives.

5. Clearly indicate the value and quality of your product or service.

   When showing a product or service, physically and emotionally involve prospective buyers in your demonstration. One tactic that always works is called the puppy sales technique. For example, while visiting a pet shop, the salesperson hands you the cute little cold nosed puppy that you were admiring, knowing that most people can't just hand the puppy back and walk out of the store. If it's impossible to have your prospective buyer physically hold your item, at least do these things:

   - Create an atmosphere that gets into the theatre of their mind while showing the advantages of ownership.
   - Emphasize value; don't just describe features.
   - Seek to discern the prospective buyer's dominant buying motive(s) while confirming his or her interests and lifestyle choices.
   - Point out how your product or service can enhance their buying choices.

6. Reduce resistance and overcome objections.

   Think through issues that may arise, especially any objections. Prepare alternative methods of response for each objection using basic techniques of conversation or third party references, *and document everything you say.*

7. Close throughout the process until final consummation is achieved.

   Closing (or consummating) a sale results from a series of minor agreements that lead to a final decision to buy. At each step, the process calls for using one trial closing question and asking at least one closing question with a call to action. If handled correctly, you'll face only four possible closing scenarios of any value: a purchase agreement, an interim decision that may lead to a purchase decision, an appointment to return for specific objectives, or the right to follow-up. Keep in mind the ABC rule—Always Be Closing (Consummating.)

8. Follow up by keeping in contact with your prospects.

   Earn the right to follow up with all prospective buyers. Keep in contact until the prospect purchases from you or someone else. Maintain complete prospect profile records with specified reasons for contacting those people. As always, record any results achieved.

9. Serve well and you will sell well.

   Customers can sense when you have their best interests at heart. That's why you're wise to service your customers before, during, and after the sale. Prepare them to maintain reasonable expectations about the buying and implementation processes. Communicate with them at least once a week, always being informed and informative. Practice these basic fundamentals to fight the plague of complacency and improve your sales skills, and you will see results.

ANTICIPATE AND RESOLVE ISSUES
BEFORE THEY BECOME PROBLEMS!

"Ordinary people believe only in the possible. Extraordinary people visualize not what is possible or probable, but rather what is impossible. And by visualizing the impossible, they begin to see it as possible."

—*Cherie Carter-Scott*

Chapter 2

Create the Desire to Buy

As previously mentioned, there's a logical sequence to effective selling:

1. You build rapport,
2. You identify a need or problem, and
3. You present a solution.

Handled properly, this powerful sequence creates a "buy from me, today, at my price" mood. But creating that mood and sensing your buyer's inner motivation takes empathy and good communication skills.

Consider, for example, that the average American male doesn't like to shop. Therefore, you'd approach male prospects in a happy, optimistic, open manner. Attempt to make an emotional connection with them and when you do, look for their mood to transform. It's an important step to take to get the result you want: *buying from you, today, at your price.*

Create the Right Mood

Gentle selling can be as powerful (or more so) as *pressure selling*; *slow motion selling* usually works better than *high-speed selling*. It's important that both you and your entire sales team understand these concepts. Gentle selling is listening to what the prospective buyer wants. I find that it's easy just to ask the prospect, "Please tell me how you like to make a major purchase?" Prospective buyers will give you a roadmap to how they want to be sold—so follow it.

I begin my seminars with a question. "How many of you like to buy something–anything for yourself or a loved one?" About ninety-nine percent of the people raise their hands. Then I ask, "How many of you like to have a sales person get in your face and sell–sell–sell?" Nobody raises their hand! If people do not appreciate that type of selling why do we teach our staff to sell that way?

Create an atmosphere where people want to buy from you and referrals will come flowing toward your company and you as a salesperson.

Remember, prospects don't care who does what in the sales process. All they remember is the atmosphere that you as a group created. One person on your team can offer them coffee; another can take their kids to watch videos or color in a coloring book, and so on. In this environment, if you don't make the sale today, your prospects will be happy to come back because they don't feel intimidated—and you won't have to start rapport-building all over again. Compare this approach with turning your prospects over to a high-pressure manager as many direct sales firms do. Rarely do prospects come back or invite you back to their office when they feel emotionally pinned to the wall.

If you and your sales team have created the right, non-threatening, relaxed climate and you've honed your listening skills, prospects will tell you what they didn't like about a competing company and their personnel. All too often, they point out their dislike for the pressure-filled, high-speed actions of the salespeople—and you can learn from that.

Remember to answer every one of their questions with enthusiasm, which also sets the mood you want. Henry Ford said, "Enthusiasm is the yeast that makes your hopes rise to the stars. Enthusiasm is the spark in your eyes, the swing in your gait, the grip of your hand, the irresistible surge of your will and your energy to execute your ideas. Enthusiasts are fighters, they have fortitude, and they have staying qualities.

Enthusiasm is at the bottom of all progress! With it, there is accomplishment. Without it, there are only alibis."

EMOTIONS ARE CONTAGIOUS.
ANSWER EVERY QUESTION WITH ENTHUSIASM.

Make Your Presentations Effective

As long as people have been analyzing the selling process, a running controversy has raged over the use of "canned" presentations—those made up of rote descriptions delivered in a manner that mesmerizes the listener in the shortest possible time.

1. Plan your presentations carefully.

Of course, your presentations—like your answers to questions—should be well planned and thought out. A carefully organized presentation takes a great deal of preparation. But the selling process still begins with an emotional connection, which can be extremely difficult to achieve when an elaborate "canned" presentation requires your total concentration.

Advocates of a "canned" presentation point out that new salespeople can memorize it in less time than it takes to develop their own. They argue that using one that's already prepared gets them selling more quickly, which helps them initially make enough sales to cover their basic income needs. Make sure, however, that you don't let this approach *replace* an effective, client-oriented sales presentation!

Remember, once you've built rapport, your next step is to determine the features and benefits prospects want to hear about during the more formal part of your presentation. That means you can't plan every exact word in detail. Instead, show that you're knowledgeable about your product or service and the value it offers. Relax. Given the right mental and emotional setup, you'll have the right words available to you when you need them.

2. Learn from the masters of selling.

Highly successful sales people with years of experience say they don't prepare for their sales presentations. But this is rarely true. While experienced salespeople may distribute their preparation time differently than less experienced ones, they still prepare!

One form is by successfully mastering "people watching." They understand people, they ask questions, and they listen. They expertly discover problems and identify dominant buying motives. They know their product/service so thoroughly that, almost magically, they can zero in on features and benefits that best appeal to their current prospects. And people love to buy from them because they're "the experts"—and because they trust them.

So what do master salespeople do to prepare? They gather information about the marketplace and their competitors. They research their competitors on the Internet, using the company's Web site which often contains the company's mission statement, financial data, and names of executive officers, including the board of directors. This information provides insight into the company.

A master salesperson will be sure to talk with knowledgeable people in their competitor's marketing department, for many employees love to talk about their company. Sometimes an aide or secretary will even reveal problems the company is having with another competitor's product. Especially if you are new to sales, gleaning ideas from the experts—and then testing them—helps you prepare well. Your only limit to developing different tactics is your own imagination.

3. Encourage customer participation.

Every presentation—no matter how it's organized or what methods are used—must get the prospect involved in the selling process. There's a saying that "average salespeople position the prospect as an uninvolved bystander; good salespeople position the prospect as an interested observer; great salespeople involve the prospect as an active participant."

What exactly is the difference? Great salespeople ensure that prospects are active in the selling and decision-making process. By contrast, when prospects get shut out of the presentation, they usually remain aloof, contributing nothing to the conversation. In this type of situation, they also buy nothing! As Confucius once said:

> Tell me and I will forget,
> Show me and I will remember,
> Involve me and I will understand.

Your sales success depends on making sure your prospects understand the process of buying, what they're buying, and the benefits they're receiving. As a clincher, they must believe and agree that the benefits provided by your service/product are more important than keeping the money it takes to buy it.

Creating understanding starts by asking questions and then listening to—and understanding—the prospect's answers. Beyond asking questions yourself, encourage your prospects to ask questions about various features of your product/service, responding to them with honesty and enthusiasm. This approach is so vital that sales seminars spend considerable time getting students to organize and role-play the questions asked during the presentation as a way to gain maximum participation.

4. Be active, focus on benefits, and involve prospects in dreaming.

Let's say you're selling furniture. How would you approach it? You would show your prospects the different styles and materials available, tell them about the warranty you offer and your return policy. You'd involve them by having them sit on the sofa and at the kitchen table. You'd get them to examine the design features. Then you'd explain how the furniture is constructed, comparing its construction to similar pieces sold by competitors.

Especially when selling high-ticket items, demonstrating their features and emphasizing their benefits is an absolute must. The value of this approach is based on well-researched findings that *people buy benefits rather than features!*

Perhaps even more important is being aware and knowing that people first buy because of how they feel, and then they rationalize their choices using their logic. You can make this type of rationalization easier by fully explaining the benefits your product/service provides. Knowing the many benefits also makes it easier for prospects to justify the purchase to other family members and friends—which helps prevent both buyer's remorse and product returns.

5. Facts tell, stories sell.

Tap into the powerful sales technique of painting a mind picture. A storytelling approach works because the human mind thinks in pictures, not in words. Continuing with the example of selling furniture, help your prospects create a mind image of enjoying an evening of relaxation feeling comfortable on the new sofa. Experiment by using these conversation starters that will give them a feel for this approach.

- Create a story about how wonderful it is to kick back on the sofa after an evening meal.
- Get them to dream out loud about how they'd find it easier to entertain guests.
- Get the family to tell you details about the colors they like best for the furniture pieces and the rooms they go in.
- Paint a picture of the first party they'd have after putting the furniture in place. Get them discussing who they'd invite to the party so they can picture all of their friends and family enjoying good food and company in a comfortable environment.

In short, asking specific questions can bring your sales presentation to life. By actively involving your prospects, you reinforce concepts, create powerful mental images and emotions, build rapport, and create a desirable mood—*I want to buy from you, today, at your price.*

YOU'VE WORKED HARD SO FAR;
DON'T LOSE THE SALE HERE!

Emphasize Benefits as well as Features

Features are both the tangible and intangible qualities of your product or service. They're facts that don't change, no matter who buys what you're selling.

Using the selling of a home as an example, its tangible features include the carpet, insulation, paint color, and anything that can be detected through one of the five senses. Most product manufacturers provide a video that is extremely useful in demonstrating features. Its intangible features include the service you and your company provide after purchasing the home you're selling. Keep in mind that exceptionally good service is rare. Selling your product/service at a fair profit and then providing more service than your customers expect, builds customer loyalty and brings future referral. After all, most people want their friends and family to be taken care of too.

Benefits, by contrast, make up the perceived value or worth that individuals believe they will derive from purchasing your service/product. Because benefits are by definition subjective, the perceived benefits that buyers will enjoy from purchasing your product/service can differ from buyer to buyer.

The alert salesperson studies, observes, and listens to what his or her prospects say. Salespeople stress the benefits of each feature appropriately in terms the prospective buyers would use. Every feature has numerous benefits. Remember, one feature doesn't equal one benefit. Listen to your prospects and custom communicate the benefits based on their needs. *Don't sell to your own standards; sell to theirs!*

What differentiates a professional salesperson from others? It's the ability to translate features into benefits. Even if you know which features can fulfill a buyer's motive, you must "connect the dots" for your prospective buyers in a meaningful way.

That means to effectively translate! You know your product/service better than they do, so you have to translate the features into the benefits that they want. Use expressions like "what this means to you is…" or "this will allow you to…" Your words are designed to accomplish one purpose: connect features and benefits in the minds of your potential buyers. Properly done, this approach answers an underlying question every prospect asks: "What's in it for me?"

TRANSLATING FEATURES INTO BENEFITS
HELPS YOU
GAIN A NECESSARY COMMITMENT TO BUY.

Get a Commitment to Buy

Before you can gain your prospective buyer's commitment, however, you must secure agreement that your solution will solve their problems. An agreement is essential. Remember, people like to participate in agreements; they never like to be told.

This "nail down," as it is sometimes called, is an essential step in building units of commitment. It's based on your prospective buyer's agreement. Checking on your prospective buyer's understanding and agreement throughout your presentation is part of the "nail down" process and helps ensure progress toward closing or consummating a sale.

To do this, you'd normally ask a series of questions to which the prospect can be expected to answer, "Yes." Suppose, however, that you ask, "You agree with me on this, don't you?" and the prospect says, "No, I don't," what would you do? *Realize you're in a better position now than before you asked the question because suddenly you've become aware you have a problem.* Had you not found out about this lack of agreement, you would have pushed on to the close and probably failed to make the sale. So find the source of the problem you've been warned about and correct it. Then ask another "nail down" question. Move forward only when agreements between you have been reached.

PEOPLE LIKE TO PARTICIPATE IN AGREEMENTS;
THEY NEVER LIKE TO BE TOLD.

Stress Value Over Price

Great salespeople focus on price only when the well has gone dry.

How many product categories in America are led by the lowest-price brand? The answer is "zero." Therefore, how much profit can you realize in selling a product/service at the lowest price? The answer is "barely more than zero." The truth is people don't care about price nearly as much as they care about value. For example:

- Maytag introduced the Neptune washing machine at nearly twice the price of a conventional washer, and it quickly became the number-two-selling washer in America. Why? Because people are extremely interested in the benefits, that saving both money and energy offers them. The customer's perception of this is this machine offers a great *value*.
- Gillette introduced the Fusion, a revolutionary new five blade shaving system for the closest shave ever in fewer strokes with little or no irritation. It is the most expensive razor and the best selling one. Why? Because what Gillette sells the benefit of a comfortable and close shave. They do not dwell on the price.

PEOPLE DON'T CARE ABOUT PRICE NEARLY AS MUCH AS THEY CARE ABOUT VALUE.

Final Win-Win Negotiations

The process of negotiation is simply this: seeking to reach an agreement based on mutual interest. With that as your goal, never put your prospects in a win/lose position during a negotiation! Instead, use a proven win/win strategy in which both parties seek solutions that bring mutual gain. If you successfully develop and use a win-win negotiating strategy, you can walk through your community with your head up, do follow-up visits to your customers, and have them thank you for selling to them. When all that is in place, you can graciously ask your customers for referrals—and receive them with pleasure.

ALWAYS USE A WIN/WIN STRATEGY.

"This is where Henry quit training our sales staff."

"Stop selling. Start helping."

—Zig Ziglar

Chapter 3
The Power of Questions

Asking proper questions encourages prospective buyers to tell you what you need to know to create a "buy from you, today, at your price" mood. When you combine powerful questions with effective listening skills, you'll have the power and means to uncover needs and formulate responses that move your prospects toward a buying decision.

You'll never accomplish this, however, by using a form or printed questionnaire to ask questions. Although many companies have a computer follow-up program that asks for certain information, this type of questioning rarely, if ever, helps you sell your product or service. While the data collected in questionnaires may be good for follow-up, you can also secure the same data talking with buyers, listening, and writing down information. Indeed, this manner seems less intimidating than answering a questionnaire and, perhaps more important, it helps establish rapport. Remember, buyers don't want to be interrogated; they're engaged with you because they *have an interest in your product or service.*

Many new salespersons are surprised when their prospects don't immediately buy their product or service. Feeling self-conscious, they think perhaps it's because they—

- Aren't doing an effective job of asking questions.
- Aren't doing an effective job of listening to the buyer's cues.
- Have preconceived notions about the buyers based on the cars they drive and the clothes they wear.
- Anticipated answers, interrupted dialogue, and/or told them what they think they want to hear.
- Think they already know the answers, so they don't even bother asking questions or listening with full attention.
- Have not uncovered the true needs of the buyer (After all, how can you satisfy needs if you don't know what they are?).

During the question-asking time, it's appropriate to discover the buyer's objections and develop responses that address these objections. Through this process, you continue to establish rapport. The old adage still rings true: "You can earn a commission using techniques, but you can earn a fortune building friendships/relationships."

The most effective sales presentation is 25 percent questioning/talking and 75 percent listening. How does that compare with what you presently do? I can't tell you how many times I've heard salespeople respond to the subject of asking questions by saying something like, "That doesn't apply to what I'm selling" or, "We're different. I need to talk more and tell them about the features." Wrong! They're throwing out excuses. When salespeople respond that way, they're really saying, "I don't know how to ask questions *effectively*."

Ask Power Questions—and Know What They Are

Developing and asking power questions is the fulcrum point of a salesperson's ability to understand prospective buyers' needs. That's why I suggest you ask only open-ended questions—ones that don't elicit a "Yes" or "No" response unless you're sure that getting a "Yes" will be a slam-dunk.

Challenge yourself to examine the questions you're asking during the sales process using these questions as guides to evaluating your own (I suggest you copy this page and post it in a place where you can refer to these questions often).

1. Is the question clear and concise?

    Does the buyer understand the question, its meaning, content, and implication?

2. Does the question require productive thinking before the buyer can formulate a response?

    As a result of the question, have you put the prospect on the path toward buying your product or service today?

3. Does the question force the buyer to evaluate new infor mation about the concepts being discussed?

    Are you building credibility with prospects by asking questions that don't make them feel inferior, but will challenge them in new ways?

4. Does the question make you seem more knowledgeable than your competitors by probing in new areas?

    Are you separating yourself from the competition by asking questions the competition never thought to ask, or are you following a standard questionnaire?

5. Does the question lead the buyer to draw from past happy experiences?

    Are you asking questions that make prospects share experiences of other purchasing scenarios they've enjoyed? *These are not only sales questions; they are rapport-building questions.*

6. Does the question generate a response that the buyer has never thought of before?

    A new twist will make you appear more professional, confident, and at the top of your game—not the same old question they received from your competitor.

7. Does the question provide a tie-down answer that moves the presentation process toward a close?

    Using questions, lead-ins, or ending words like *don't you*, *isn't it*, *shouldn't you*, or *doesn't it* gives the buyer an opportunity to say "Yes" to a particular part of your presentation and allows you to move on to the next area.

8. Does the question relate directly to the buyer's buying needs?

    The more direct the question, the more likely you are to get a direct response. *This is the time to really, really listen!* The first response you hear is usually the truest response (Prospects can suddenly realize they've given you more information than they wanted to and they'll change their answers).

9. Does the question relate directly to the buyer's objective?

    Are you probing in areas to which prospects can relate and encouraging them to give truthful answers?

10. Does the question draw information from the buyer that helps make the sale easier?

    Sample questions: "What do you like about your

present product or service?" or, "What changes would you make?" or, "What are your expectations of the new product or service?" or (my favorite), "If you had $10,000 to spend, how you would change or improve our product/service?"

11. Does the question create an atmosphere that is positive and conducive to consummating the sale?

    Is the question provocative or thought provoking? Caution: You don't want to make prospects angry as the result of asking questions; rather, you want to make them think.

12. Are you asking a closing question, one that elicits a buying decision?

    My favorite question is this: "Do you have any other questions before we start the paperwork?"

I recommend that you have ten to twelve different closing questions written down, then rehearse and use them as the occasion arises. Incorporate them into your selling process. If you practice them thoroughly, I promise you two things:

1. You'll be highly challenged.
2. The reward for reflecting on these questions will make you a better salesperson—one who realizes increasingly greater financial rewards.

CHALLENGE YOURSELF AND YOUR PROSPECTS WITH THE POWER OF THE QUESTIONS YOU ASK.

To Close More Sales, Learn To Listen More

It's absolutely amazing that listening—a primary and critical skill that's needed for personal, family, and business success—is rarely taught in school. While the ability to listen effectively is arguably the most important aspect of the selling process, it's frequently the weakest of the many skills sales professionals require. How often have you asked people to repeat what they just said?

How often do you hear the statement, "You weren't listening to me"? Research on the subject of poor listening reveals the following lessons learned:

1. Be aware of the two biggest impediments to listening.
   - You've already got an opinion of what will be said before beginning to listen.
   - You've already made up your mind before hearing the full story.

2. To become a better listener, understand how you currently listen.
   - Are you doing something else when someone is speaking?
   - Do you usually think about something else when someone is speaking?
   - Are you fake listening so that you can get in your comments?

- Do you wait for a pause before responding because you already know the answer?

3. You may stop listening at one or more of these points:
   - After you have formulated your response.
   - After you have been turned off by the speaker.
   - When you have decided to interrupt to say something.
   - When the person speaking isn't saying anything you want to hear.

4. Your attitude must be conducive to effective listening.
   - Are you afraid to hear what is about to be said and thus block it out? *Never be afraid to listen!*
   - Do you take for granted the others involved—your child, spouse, co-worker and, above all, your prospect?
   - Are you preoccupied with other projects?
   - Are you just rude?
   - Do you think you know what *will* be said, thus pre judging the speaker?

Having identified some of the barriers to effective listening, here are guidelines to maximize your listening skills, increase your productivity, reduce errors, gain customer happiness, and sell more (not to mention nurture better relationships). Observe these eighteen, very critical rules in this order:

1. Listen with the intent to understand.

2. Listen with the intent to repeat.

3. Don't interrupt (i.e., "but…but…but…" or, "after that—").

4. Ask questions, and then be very, very quiet. Note: It's amazing how much we learn by just keeping quiet. Not only do people think that you are smarter if you are quiet, but you learn more by listening than by speaking.

5. Concentrate on the other person's answers, not on your own thoughts.

6. Listen without prejudging. Prejudice will distort what you hear.

7. Use eye contact and verbal feedback (i.e., um, gee, I see, oh) to show the other person you're listening.

8. Don't jump to a conclusion before you hear about the *entire* situation.

9. Listen for specific purpose, details, and any conclusions.

10. Interpret what you hear quietly or take notes.

11. Listen to what is not said. What's implied is often more important than what's spoken. Hint: Your tone of speech often reflects an implied meaning, so stay neutral.

12. Think between sentences spoken and during quiet times.

13. Digest what has and has not been said before engaging your mouth.

14. Ask clarifying questions to be sure you understood what was said or meant.

15. Ask questions to ensure the speaker has finished speaking.

16. Demonstrate that you're listening by taking action.

17. If you find yourself thinking while someone else is speaking, switch to thinking about solutions. Never embellish the problem!

18. Avoid all distractions. Turn off any cell phones or pagers, close the door, and clear your mind. Sit or stand in close proximity to the speaker.

Assess How Well You Listen

Take This Mini-Test:

Answer each question with: Rarely–Sometimes–Always

__ I allow people speaking to me to complete their sentences.

__ I make sure I understand the other person's point of view before responding.

__ I listen for the important points.

__ I try to understand the speaker's feelings.

__ I visualize the solution before speaking.

__ I consider my response before speaking and the effect it may have on the speaker.

__ I am in control, relaxed, and calm when speaking.

__ I use verbal feedback (um–gee–I see–oh).

__ I take notes when someone else is speaking.

__ I listen with an open mind. _ I listen even if the other person is not interesting.

__ I listen even if the other person is a jerk.

__ I look at the person who is speaking.

__ I am patient when I listen.

__ I ask questions to be sure I have understood.

__ I do my best to ensure that there are no distractions when I listen.

Add the number of A's (Always) and see how effective a listener you are.

Calculate your score.

How many A's (Always) did you have? Here are your results.

14–16 You are an excellent listener.

11–13 You are good, but need help in a few areas.

7–10 You are a fair listener. You probably think you know it all, but you could increase your income significantly by building your listening skills.

4–6 You are a poor listener and don't listen at all.

1–3 You are seriously in need of a hearing aid.

Once you've identified your weaknesses, I challenge you to turn any of them into "new listening goals" by substituting "I will" for "I" or "I will be" for "I am." For example, if you answered "Sometimes" for "I allow people speaking to me to complete their sentences," turn it into a goal by writing this: "I will allow people speaking to me to complete all sentences for the next thirty days." Write this goal on a Post-it note and place it on your desk or mirror.

As with all skills, effective listening requires that you practice, practice, and then practice even more. I assure you, however, that the benefits of becoming an effective listener far outweigh the effort required to acquire this valuable skill.

ALWAYS LISTENING EFFECTIVELY WILL BENEFIT YOU, YOUR FAMILY, AND YOUR BANK ACCOUNT.

"To satisfy our customers' needs, we'll give them what they want, not what we want to give them."

—Steve James

Chapter 4
Learn to Interview Well

What are prospective buyers thinking when they come into a place where you're selling a product or service? Based on my years of selling, I believe their silent voices sound something like this: "Don't try to sell me. Listen to me, value me, understand me, and let me know that you want to help me."

I think the trickiest part is letting your prospects know that you want to help them. Doing this well requires more than a passing knowledge of interviewing skills. If you intend to get to the core of the prospective buyers' needs and motivations, it requires practice and, above all, a plan. Your plan should be based on unearthing the conflict they experience between *where they are* in their current situation and *where they want to be.*

How to Deal with Dissonance

To help prospects first define and then express conflict or dissonance—and then agree to act on it—I suggest using the following interview sequence. Regard it as a game plan that can take you through the professional sales process while simultaneously helping prospects discover their own needs and motivations. More important, it will help them to recognize their own dissonance, which is the forerunner of the *buy from me today* results you want.

The following questions provide a template for how you can lead a conversation with prospective buyers.

1. Ask questions about their current situation—where they are now.

    Their answers will lead you to further questions and to an understanding of what they perceive as their desired situation. Remember, in the prospects' minds, perception is reality (You'll need that information as you close the sale later in the process).

2. Get them to talk about their desired situation—where they want to be.

    People always go through this process of defining

and understanding the dissonance in their present situation, whether they want to fill a simple or complex need. For example, when you go to a movie theater, you pass the popcorn stand in the lobby. When you smell the popcorn, you immediately assess your current situation. Smelling the popcorn might make you aware of a gap and evoke a desire that leads you to say, "If I don't buy popcorn, I won't enjoy the movie." If the negative consequences of not enjoying the popcorn seem worse than spending the money or consuming the calories, you buy it. If the gap (or dissonance) isn't there, you don't buy it. (Note that this scenario did not involve a decision about price. Professional salespeople don't let price enter into the interview process until later).

3. Help them identify and define their dissonance.

Ask questions to help them become aware of the difference between where they would like to be and where they are now.

Prospective buyers often need an outside expert to help them move through this analysis. Counseling people through these "thought" sequences helps bring clarity to their decision-making process.

4. Understand their sense of urgency.

This is extremely important to you, especially if you're sponsoring a special event. Because of the sales traffic you've generated, you have a tremendous amount of opportunity. In this situation you have to quickly decide which potential buyers are ready to make a decision. Rarely will people make a purchase decision unless they feel a sufficient sense of urgency—either for the relief of pain or the hope of gain.

5. Get them to talk about the consequences of staying where they are now and not taking action.

   The most effective salespeople know how to take the process even deeper. They find the prospective buyers' fears or reasons why they're putting off making a decision. They learn about political, personal, and/or relationship issues that affect their decisions. And they learn all they can about the payoff that their prospects want. This requires asking questions like, "Now that I understand where you would like to be versus where you are now, are you content to stay with your current situation?"

6. After asking critical questions, be quiet.

   Wait for a response. Read their body language. Listen to their emotions. Watch what they do with their hands and posture. If you're dealing with more than one person, carefully observe how they look at each other. Chances are, you'll quickly learn a great deal about their sense of urgency. You will also discover who the real decision-makers are as you see others look to them for a signal of what to do. This is when they reveal hidden fears or concerns about making a major purchase.

7. Get them to summarize the advantages and disadvantages.

   At the appropriate time, if you truly believe you can create value for your prospects, say something like, "The real questions are: What are the disadvantages of staying with your current situation versus the advantages of making this purchase?"

8. Don't try to sell to more than one prospective buyer at a time.

   An old wife's tale states it well, "Man who chases two rabbits at the same time catches neither." The more expertly you give people your full attention, ask questions, and allow your prospects to provide their own answers, the more quickly you can help them make a decision to *buy from me today!*

ASKING PROBING QUESTIONS GETS TO THE HEART OF ANY DISSONANCE PEOPLE FEEL.

"Problems are only opportunities in work clothes."

—Henry J. Kaiser

CHAPTER 5
WAYS TO DEAL WITH OBJECTIONS

There probably hasn't been a sales training class in the last twenty years that didn't talk about objections and how to overcome them. Why? *Because objections are and always will be an important part of the sales process.* Unfortunately, they can also be a significant problem, especially if they occur during the "close" cycle.

Before talking about preventing and/or responding to objections, however, understand two important facts:

Fact 1: Objections aren't going to go away.

Yet, they don't necessarily represent a problem. Objections—if handled properly—can become positive factors in helping close the sale. The operative phrase here is, *"if handled properly."*

Fact 2: There are no new objections.

Any sales professional who has been on the job six months has probably heard them all. Therefore, the vast majority of objections can be predicted and responses developed to handle these known objections. The classic number-one objection—"your price is too high"—is often used because the prospect has nothing to lose and everything to gain by saying it.

Yes, you can anticipate objections and you can either prevent them from occurring by qualifying them accurately or significantly reducing any negative impact. Sound simple? It is, but it requires preparation, practice, creativity, and focus. Your reward for this effort will be superior sales that I'm sure you know lead to a fatter wallet.

Prevent Objections

A common reaction to the "your price is too high" objection (especially from new salespeople) is to immediately reduce the selling price. Not a good idea! A far better way is to anticipate this objection and prevent it from occurring by determining your prospects' attitudes toward price during your rapport-building session.

1. Draw attention to value.

   Using selling a car as an example, you might make comments such as, "Studies have shown that the savings in fuel energy helps offset the price of a new car." You also want to talk about value, not only today but in the long run.

2. Watch for the "stall" tactic.

   What may first seem to be an objection could be a stall or delay tactic. Stalls can, and often do, have the same frustrating effect as making an objection. Prospects use this technique for a wide variety of reasons, including wanting to tell the salesperson "No" but lacking the courage or conviction to say it early in the process.

   Another stall is the "We want to think about it" statement. That usually means they're just window-shopping. They don't have the money, can't make a decision, don't trust or have confidence in the salesperson and/or selling company, and so on. Do your best to reveal these factors and overcome them during your rapport-building session.

3. Actively ask questions and listen to responses.

   Objections can often be prevented by carefully listening during the qualifying session. What are customers really looking for and how do they want to buy? Using computer sales as an example start with a question like, "Have you seen a computer that you really like?" If you get a positive response, follow up with, "May I ask why you didn't buy it?" A common answer to this question is, "I didn't like the attitude of the salesperson." If you get this response, say, "May I ask what you mean by that? I don't want to make the same mistake that person did." Then listen.

MAKING A SUPERIOR EFFORT WHEN DEALING WITH OBJECTIONS LEADS TO SUPERIOR RESULTS.

Prepare for Objections

You're sure to run into situations in which stating objections couldn't be prevented. Be both prepared and practiced, using the following techniques:

1. Identify and list all possible objections.

   Remember, there are no *new* objections. Most sales people have heard them all. Start by making a detailed list of the top ten to fifteen common objections related to your product or service.

2. Script responses and develop strategies to each objection.

   To successfully address objections, get prepared. Brainstorm and create several scenarios for each objection. While it may take time to complete this task, ask other salespeople (including your sales manager) to help. In fact, I suggest you make this a learning exercise during a sales meeting.

3. Develop tools that enhance and support your responses.

   Testimonials, letters, comparison charts, and third-party testing reports can reduce the number of objections and enhance rapport as you move toward the close process.

4. Rehearse your scripts by role-playing.

   After you've written your responses, schedule several role-playing sessions to get familiar with each one and make them sound natural. This can become another effective exercise for a sales meeting.

5. Refine your responses.

   After you role-play with other members of your sales team, you'll likely want to revise some of your responses. As if you were in a Broadway play, you have to rehearse and tweak them well before you're in front of a real prospect. *Never rehearse on your prospective buyers.* If you do, you set yourself up for failure!

6. Make final revisions based on real-world situations.

   No matter how many times you revise and rehearse your answers, real-world situations will often dictate that you make changes. Document these changes and, if appropriate, share them with the other salespeople as a learning tool.

7. Keep your scripts/responses in a master notebook.

   If you are a sales manager, give each salesperson a copy of your notebook. When a new salesperson joins your staff, he or she then has an in-house sales training manual—one that will provide insights, techniques, and eventually, income.

8. Meet regularly to discuss revisions.

   A major criticism of many industries is that they've been using the same selling techniques for the past thirty plus years. *Keep your responses fresh with new terminology, and continually update the benefits of your service/product.*

9. Hone a rainbow of skills.

   Remember that no matter how well you prepare and practice your responses to objections, your overall sales success lays primarily in these areas:

   - Knowledge of effective selling skills, especially the concept of dissonance.
   - Knowledge of your service or product.
   - Knowledge of your prospective buyers.
   - Relationship with your prospective buyers.
   - Creativity.

- Attitude.
- Sincere desire to help your prospective buyers.
- Persistence. Note that none of these have to do with price. While some may be related to cost, they all have to do with value.

PREPARE, PRACTICE, AND REFINE YOUR VALUE-BASED RESPONSES TO OBJECTIONS.

Responding to the Emotional Side of Objections

Objections are nothing more than the rungs up the ladder to consummating the sale. You climb this ladder by grasping each rung and overcoming them one at a time. Think of objections as statements from your prospects that they want or need to know more. As such, they are required ingredients in the selling recipe.

All of us have emotions. Dr. Stephen Post has written a great book, *Why Good Things Happen to Good People.* In his book he states that science has proven that people that give and share their emotions are happier people. Understand that your prospective buyers are just expressing their emotions through the spoken word.

Two types of objections emerge: minor and major. A minor objection tells you that a prospect is just trying to slow down the purchase decision. "Hey, take it slower; I need some time to think." A major objection is referred to as a condition. Many times when working with couples, for example, one spouse brings up a "condition" and the other spouse explains it to you.

Unless your prospects are dealing with extreme conditions that would prohibit the sale, raising objections are ways they allow their emotions to begin taking over. They may be ready to buy emotionally, but their logical reasoning side shouts to be more cautious. Realize that this is normal. Because of the discomfort they feel, objections often don't sound like a polite request for more information. As a professional, you learn to recognize this and know what to do about it.

In fact, you should smile inside when you hear an objection. It gives you a chance to address their concerns and provide information they need to put their fears to rest. It also slows down the pace, which can help build a more secure relationship.

To respond to their emotional objections, follow these steps:

1. Hear them out.
2. Feed the objection back.
3. Question the objection.
4. Answer the objection.
5. Confirm the answer.
6. Attempt a test close.

7. Finalize the sale if the test close receives a positive response.

The following will help you examine these concepts in more detail:

1. Answer their need for rationalization.

Objections can sometimes be a cry for help; a need to be more convinced that the investment is wise, safe, and within their budget. Price objections almost always fit into this category, creating a trap into which many salespeople fall. Why do prospects question price? They may feel obligated to "deal" as a matter of pride or simply an attempt to "feel you out." Most prospects think, "By objecting to price, I have nothing to lose." The professional sales person realizes this and attempts to shift the focus to quality; e.g., helping prospects understand they're getting an even greater value than they first thought.

2. Respond to their desire for support.

Emotion-based objections can be addressed by getting more support material to help convince others—family, associates, and neighbors—who are likely to question the buyers' decision. As a professional salesperson, it's critical that you give those prospects more than enough "comeback" information so they can justify their purchase decision.

3. Discern if they want to sidestep the real reason.

   Some people simply like to hear themselves talk, while others will make silly statements just to throw you off guard. For example, in the middle of your presentation, your prospect might say, "Oh, I see you didn't finish talking about the inside of your product." Or the person may suddenly look up and remark, "I wonder how you clean it." While objections like these often represent blowing smoke, treat them as seriously as any others.

   How do you know what's really important to your prospect? First, never take objections at face value, nor take them personally. Instead, search for the real message that's often obscured by the turndown. When you take the objection literally and give up, you not only lose the sale, but you've actually done your prospect a disservice if you really believe in your product and your company.

4. Know the difference between a condition and an objection.

   The most common condition is having no money, no credit, or bad credit. No matter how great the opportunity may be, if prospects can't qualify, there's no point spending your valuable time with them. You're better off working with qualified buyers.

   Remember, the main purpose of qualifying your prospects is to determine whether any conditions exist that will make a final agreement impossible. Don't waste anyone's time trying to overcome impossible conditions. Instead, show genuine interest and concern, even if it takes a few more minutes of your time. And when they leave, send a thank-you note and ask for referrals. You have invested your time in this prospect; try to get a return on this investment through future referrals.

5. Practice, practice, practice.

   Think of and write down a response for each of the objections stated below. Practice your answers and be prepared to give them in the right situations.

   1. A retailer up the street has the same product but it's cheaper.
   2. We want to look a little longer.
   3. My uncle is in this business, and he said your brand of product is not well built.
   4. Can't you lower your price? The supplier up the street gave me a lower price.
   5. The interest you offer on a purchase loan is __ percent. Why is yours so high?
   6. We want our first year's payments to be interest free.
   7. Can't you put the down payment in my selling price?

8. In short, objections are an integral part of sales. Learn to expect and to respond to them.

BACK DOWN THE LADDER CAREFULLY,
LEAVING IT IN PLACE FOR FUTURE USE.

"Quality begins on the inside...and then works its way out."

—Bob Moawad

Chapter 6
The Pricing Issue

During my seminars, I ask the audiences if they'd like me to prove the claim "price is seldom the reason for buying or not buying." I simply ask, "Is there anybody here who has purchased any item solely because it was the cheapest?" No one has ever raised his or her hand.

The point is clear! Many factors go into a buying decision, and price is only one of those factors. But price is almost never the main criterion; something else is. And it's your job as a professional salesperson to find the real concern and address it effectively.

According to a reliable study, ninety four percent of sales in the United States are determined by factors other than price. Follow-up surveys with customers who negotiated long and hard over price turned up a surprising fact: These same customers based their buying decisions on such non-price factors such as suitability, convenience, reputation, and professional attitude of the salesperson (including that person's ability to listen). Not surprisingly, the salesperson's ability to understand the potential buyer's needs exceeded the price factor in importance.

Never Argue or Defend Your Prices

This survey offers important clues about how to influence a sale. For example, when dealing with price, never argue or defend your prices. Instead, probe gently and professionally to find out the real reason for buyer hesitation. Use the "Feel, Felt, Found" Sales Method that experienced salespeople use effectively. After listening to a prospective buyer, state, "I understand why you feel that way, because many of my customers have felt that way before they found out all the information." At this point in the sale, have all supporting documents ready to verify what you just stated. I suggest that you show them the documentation while making that statement. This will gain you tremendous credibility.

Realize that, in the process of asking questions to uncover needs accurately, you position yourself as an expert consultant for your product or service. During your discussion, focus on the value of your product or service rather than getting drawn into an argument over price. Keep emphasizing the benefits that address the concerns you've already learned are important to the potential buyer.

IF A PRODUCT OR SERVICE FAILS TO PROMISE A BENEFIT, IT'S USUALLY NOT WORTH BUYING.

The Person Who Asks the Question Has Control

A professional salesperson realizes that questions about price are buying signals rather than objections. For example, when a potential buyer says, "Your price is too high," you might respond with a question such as, "Why do you say that?" When you ask a question, pause and remain perfectly silent until the potential buyer replies. Then whenever possible, follow with another question and again remain silent, allowing the person to answer. Keep in mind that if you ask good questions, it may take a few moments for the buyer to justify any preconceived opinions and give you an answer that's truthful.

If the potential buyer then says, "I can't afford it," gently ask something like, "Why do you feel that way when the lender qualified you for this amount?" or, "How far apart are we on the price?" Lean forward attentively and wait for an answer.

Potential buyers rarely have ready answers to these questions. But by asking the questions, you not only maintain control over the flow of the sales conversation, you're likely to learn the real reason behind any hesitation to buy.

YOUR GOAL IS TO UNEARTH REAL OBJECTION OTHER THAN PRICE.

Don't Discuss Price Out of Place

Beware! If you engage in a price discussion before the potential buyer thoroughly understands the benefits and advantages of your product or service, *you will usually lose the sale!*

I understand that some people walk in the front door and ask only one question: "How much is that?" But if you give in to the temptation to state the price immediately, you'll spend valuable prospecting time justifying the price you just stated.

Instead, your response might be, "I know price is important to you. Would you sit down first to discuss your particular needs? When I have a clear understanding of your current situation, then I'll be better able to assist you in making the best decision."

Sometimes potential buyers will insist that you state the price before allowing any discussion to proceed. When faced with a demand like that, counter with, "I don't know what the total may be."

"What do you mean, you don't know?" the potential buyer might ask.

You'd reply, "I don't know what other costs may be involved until I learn more about your needs."

Once you postpone the price discussion, you can go

into a questioning process, fully positioning yourself as a professional salesperson.

Occasionally, shoppers may demand to know the price before you have a chance to discuss their needs or before they even know what you are selling. If you state a price, you'll invariably get a response like, "We can't afford that," or, "It's too expensive." *At this moment, you are in great and immediate danger of losing the sale.*

Most likely, the potential buyers have a price in mind that's based on what a relative or friend paid for a similar product or service years ago—long before recent price increases. Or they may have a certain amount in their budget that they can pay monthly. Once you have discovered that number (as long as it's reasonably close to what you're asking), you can demonstrate that the difference in price is more than made up by the increased value of your product or service and the follow-up service. Frequently reassure them by saying things like, "This is a great price," or, "This is an excellent product or service for your needs. I know you'll be very happy with it."

Customers today don't want the lowest price. They've had enough experience with low-price items to know that low-quality items, products, or services frequently cause more problems than they cure. Above all they want to go home thinking the opposite of being taken advantage of—they want to feel part of a win-win situation. Your goal is to insure that they leave feeling good about having purchased your product or service at a fair price and at a fair commission. These are the customers who will give you referrals—the life-blood for professional sale people.

CUSTOMERS DON'T WANT THE LOWEST PRICE;
THEY WANT A FAIR PRICE.

Be Proud of Your Prices

What's the most important aspect of dealing professionally with the price issue? You should be proud of your prices and know the prices of your top three competitors, and then you can justify your prices. Prospective buyers are not always looking for the lowest price they are looking for the best value. Always remember that the question of price is not an objection; it's a buying signal. People like to ask that age-old question, "Is that your best price?" If your answer makes sense to them, then they will proceed. That will be true for your potential customer, too.

"Henry's doing his sales pitch again."

"It is not your customers' job to remember you. It is your obligation and responsibility to make sure they don't have a chance to forget you."

—Patricia Fripp

Chapter 7
Consummating (Closing) the Sale

Please note the use of the phrase "consummating the sale" instead of the traditional term "closing the sale." "Closing a sale" implies that "I'm now going to get aggressive to get the customer to say yes." Clearly you don't want to be remembered as a hard-close salesperson.

The dictionary's definition of consummating is "perfect ending." A perfect ending means that both you and your customers have won! That is, they have given you their money;

you have given them a product or a service of great value. This is the first step in customer satisfaction—a step that leads to referrals and more prospects for you to convert into sales. Your eventual goal is to get your customers to say "thank you" every time they see you. This professionalism in action is what separates professional salespeople from order takers.

Consummating the sale depends on several factors discussed below. To succeed, it's critical to understand the most common issues involved in consummating a sale.

Be a Team Leader

Because of the many complexities of both today's society and rapidly changing technology, the selling of both products and services leans toward team selling (discussed in Chapter 14). The salesperson assumes the role of a team leader who engages different players within the company to deliver the product or service for the customer. This being said, it's critical that you know, can trust, and are able to work with the other professionals required to successfully "consummate the sale" and satisfactorily deliver the product or service to your customer.

To effectively consummate a sale, a sales professional—

- Is a team player.
- Has patience.
- Maintains a relatively low profile.
- Has the ability to help prospects rationalize the decision that they want to make.

- Is able to develop trust from prospective buyers.
- Is able to help prospects head off procrastination, deal with fear, and bring issues out in the open for discussion.
- Can sell without gimmicks (Gimmicks are a turn-off to most prospects).
- Loves his or her job (A positive attitude is infec tious, and the money will follow).
- Has a ready and polite response when a prospect starts to stall.
- Taps into at least three gentle ways of relieving pressure.
- Is able to overcome a prospect's feeling of insecurity.

CONSUMMATING A SALE MEANSMAKING
A COMMITMENT TO DO WHAT CUSTOMERS EXPECT.

Test Prospects' Readiness to Buy

By definition, a successful sell ends with a signed contract or sales agreement. The sensitive question, therefore, "Is the prospect ready to sign?" Using the following techniques will help you determine that.

1. Ask questions.

   As a way of making this critical judgment, use a question format at the end of your statements; e.g., "don't you agree?" In addition, phrase questions in a way that will elicit a "yes" answer most of the time. The four most commonly used questions for this are:

- Isn't it…?
- Doesn't it…?
- Don't you agree that…?
- Wouldn't you like…?

You can use these questions in the front, middle, or end of your sales presentation. Your goal is to get the "yes" momentum going.

While some of the best buying signs come from questions posed by your prospects, be careful not to answer them with merely a "yes" or "no." If you do, you may back yourself in a corner with no place to go. Instead, ask the questions back to your prospects by rephrasing them. This verifies that you understood what they want. Rephrasing the question also makes it softer and gentler than a harsh-sounding "yes" or "no" answer.

2. Write down information.

After a few of these buying questions, try for a test close. One approach is to say, "Let me make a note of that." Then start filling out the purchase agreement, credit application, and whatever other papers you need. Remember, a successful sale starts with a signed purchase agreement, not an application.

3. Pay attention to body language.

   Watch your prospects' body language, which will indicate both interest and a willingness to proceed with the sale. For example, are they leaning toward you, silently asking for a reason to buy? My favorite place to watch is the person's eyes. Professional poker players wear sunglasses to prevent their opponents from seeing both the corners and pupils of their eyes. The corners turn upward and the pupils of the eyes enlarge when someone's excited. This uncontrollable reaction often happens when a prospective buyer is ready to make a purchase. The next time you're at a party where gifts are given, observe the person's eyes when receiving each gift. Or the next time you're at the mall, observe your spouse's eyes when passing a favorite shop.

4. Show genuine enthusiasm until the close.

   At this critical stage, indicate your full and genuine enthusiasm right to the end. You can show this by varying the speed and volume of your voice. You can develop and use a planned pause as if you forgot what you were saying. Most of the time, your prospects will help you finish your thoughts. In this way, you have just involved them in helping you consummate the sale. They are buying a product or service instead of being sold. Remember, everybody loves to buy; nobody likes to be sold.

STRIVE TO BE REMEMBERED AS A SALESPERSON WHO WORKED WELL WITH CUSTOMERS.

"One of the things I learned the hard way was that it doesn't pay to get discouraged. Keeping busy and making optimism a way of life can restore your faith in yourself."

—Lucille Ball

Chapter 8

Think Like A Winner

Over the years, thousands of successful people have been asked, "What do you think about most of the time?" Their answers tend to be extremely similar: *Successful people think about what they want and how to get it.* As a result of this mental focus, these people tend to accomplish more than the average person, even though they may have started with no particular advantages.

Contrast these winning thought processes with those of unsuccessful people who tend to think and talk about what they *don't* want. They dwell on the people they're mad at or who's to blame for their problems and failures. They can't understand why their lives don't improve, even though they may have been working as long and as hard as those who realize success.

In his study of more than 300,000 people, Dr. Martin Seligman of the University of Pennsylvania found that successful people are more optimistic 71% of the time than unsuccessful people. They have a positive mental attitude toward themselves, toward their relationship with God, toward others, and toward their *industries or professions.*

This last finding particularly interested me because I've come across far too many salespeople who hold a negative opinion about their own profession. I probably feel this way, because I have always considered professional selling as an honorable profession.

His further findings indicated that one's optimism was also a predictor of how happy, healthy, and wealthy they'd be—as well as how long they'd live. The conclusion: *The more optimistic and positive you are, the more energy and enthusiasm you'll have.* Your immune system will be stronger, you'll be more resistant to disease and infection, you'll get along on less sleep, and you'll have more mental and physical energy throughout the day.

In addition, the more optimistic you are, the more creative you'll likely be. You'll more consistently come up with good ideas and recognize new possibilities, including ways to get reluctant prospects to buy from you and consummate a sale. Scientific research supports the thesis that becoming a more optimistic person in every part of your life will do more to ensure your success and happiness than any other single quality that you can develop.

Think Optimistically—It's Your Job

For all the reasons stated above, it's your job (and mine) to keep thinking optimistically and remain positive *most of the time.* Yes, I said "most of the time." Like you, I know full well the disappointment of losing a sale or having a prospect fail to show up for an appointment or being assured your prospects have credit worthiness, only to find out that their attorney has told them their credit was okay *because they had filed for bankruptcy.*

Think of it this way: If you didn't have mind-boggling problems, you wouldn't be in sales—you'd be order taking, which doesn't ever pay well. So how do you train yourself to meet the problems that slap you in the face every day? You think like a winner.

ATTITUDES ARE CONTAGIOUS.
ARE YOURS WORTH CATCHING?

Practice Specific Exercises

Developing a positive attitude, like developing yourself physically, takes work. Additionally, you have to like yourself before you can expect other people to like you. Like physical fitness, you can hone optimism by practicing specific exercises continually until you automatically respond in a positive, constructive way to whatever happens to you. Here are four effective techniques to adopt:

1. Adopt and practice a future-orientated vision.

Having a future orientation in life is a common characteristic of successful people, especially those who rise to positions of leadership and responsibility in work, in society, and in their personal lives. Specifically, studies show that all great leaders have a vision of where they're going.

Leaders develop a vision not only for themselves, but also for their families and organizations—whether they own the business or work as an employee. They have the talent to visualize an ideal future and then they work to make it a reality.

Future-oriented people think about where they're heading instead of where they've been or where they are at present. They continually think about what's possible in the months and years ahead, rather than focus on the past that can't be changed.

2. Clearly state your vision.

I had the pleasure of speaking to professionals from a major real estate firm at their annual meeting. The firm's founder and president spoke of the company's future and his plans to take it exactly where it should go. He discussed the trying times facing the housing industry and how the company planned to counteract the downturn. Like a great leader, he clearly communicated his vision and invited the people who work for him to willingly join him in growing this company.

How can you be future-oriented? Simple. Ask this question: "If your life was perfect five years from now, what would it look like?" Future-oriented people can immediately answer this question because they spend lots of time thinking about it. They also think about the future consequences of their daily actions. They continually ask questions like, "If I do everything I promised on today's sale, will I get at least one more referral? If I don't do everything I promised, what will it cost me?" Do you see how future-oriented individuals assess tomorrow's possible consequences based on today's actions?

In contrast, present-oriented and past-oriented individuals think very differently. Their visions of the future tend to be vague, fuzzy. They seldom think about the future in detail. If you ask them to describe their personal goals or their company's goals, they often become defensive or resentful.

The question at this point is which attitude do you prefer for yourself?

3. Practice idealization.

When you use the idealization technique, you continually imagine the perfect outcome or solution for any situation in your life. To start, project forward three to five years and create a mental picture of the kind of life and career that would be ideal in every aspect. *Make this vision as detailed as possible!*

While idealizing your perfect future, let your mind float freely. Imagine that you have no limitation on what you can do, be, or have. Assume you have all the knowledge, experience, money, and resources you need—that all opportunities and possibilities are open to you.

Now, develop a dream list. Write down everything you'd like to have in your future and your work, as if each one were completely guaranteed. Dig deep as you answer this question: "If you had all the time and money you wanted, and if you could be or have anything in your life, what would you really want?" The greater the clarity and detail you can impart to this vision, the more powerful it becomes as a guide to your future success.

In your quest for success, however, remind yourself that it's more than making money. *It also means doing the best you can with what you have.* Success comes primarily from the doing, not just from the getting. As the great philosopher Thomas Carlyle wrote, "Let each become all that he was created capable of being." What a great definition of success!

Life challenges you every day to develop your capabilities to the fullest. Meet these challenges by developing an optimistic, future-oriented mindset—the best goal you could select. The time to start this exciting, life-changing journey into the future is now.

4. Program yourself for success.

Few people have any concept of what a marvelous gift the conscious mind actually is. Few can describe it, and even fewer can alter it. But without knowing, people wander through the deserted halls of dreams, always hoping but rarely achieving. In the realm of sales, I call this the "hoping" sales method: Hoping that somebody with good credit, a large down payment, and a ready-to-buy-today attitude will approach you. Yes, these kinds of buyers are out there, but they rarely visit your office or worst you fail to recognize or attempt to close them. Why? *Because you have to program your mind and body to seek them out and that's rarely done!*

"If you don't believe that prospects will buy, they won't." While doing research for this book and my seminars I have found that fifty-one percent of the people that either come to your office or schedule an appointment for you to visit them will buy your product within six months. Only fifteen percent are wasting your time. The other thirty-four percent will buy sometime later. My question is, are you striving to close the fifty-one percent and effectively following up on the thirty-four percent? Have you ever heard this self-fulfilling prophecy? I've met numerous salespeople who engage in this type of negative thinking. Sure enough, they're always right. *Nobody is buying!* At least, not from them!

TO GO FROM FAILURE TO SUCCESS, STOP NEGATIVE THINKING BY CHANGING YOUR MINDSET.

Train Your Conscious Mind

One definition of the conscious mind is: "the part that thinks, and the place where ideas form." You bring information into this part of your mind through the five senses of sight, smell, touch, hearing, and taste. Your free will also resides here. So does your concept of pain, pleasure, and—yes—self-imposed limitations.

Remember, lack and limitation can exist only when you make room for them in your mind. You become what you think about, preceded by images in your mind. Therefore, it will help you to program your mind to think positive thoughts about a wide variety of subjects—your job, your family, and your community—by gaining insight into this marvelous creation called the conscious mind.

Understand these Sectors.

To better explain the concept of the conscious mind, I've divided it into six parts or sectors I call *reason, imagination, will, intuition, memory, and perception.*

Reason—You have the ability to accept or reject any thought and to make decisions. Many people, however, choose not to use or develop this mental sector. In selling homes, for example, you'd say, "When considering the pride of home ownership, the tax advantage, and the security it offers a family, it stands to *reason* that everybody should own a home."

Imagination—There is a power flowing into and within each person that allows the creation of great and wonderful ideas. It's more powerful than all the nuclear energy present in the world today. Imagine if the founders of great companies and builders of great communities had limited their thinking and dreaming. Yet, imagination is probably one of the most underused resources on the planet.

Use your imagination to envision everyone living in an energy-efficient home in a beautiful community, or everyone driving a new vehicle with the latest safety equipment, *and knowing that you made this possible.* Take that thought and decide what you have to do to make your dream a reality in your market. *Yes, I said you.* What have you done to improve the image of your particular industry? Do you support and vote for candidates who favor your industry in elections? Do you participate in the local or state association for your industry? Get involved—and let your imagination take you places.

Will—Perhaps better known as will power, this part of the conscious mind allows you to concentrate. Some people are easily taken off course because they haven't developed this critical mind sector. Yet, you do have the power to mentally focus on your goals and to never be taken off track, despite current circumstances, environments, or situations.

This part of the mind also gives you the discipline to acutely listen to what your prospects tell you. When you listen with the intent to completely understand what they're saying, they will describe the product or service they want to purchase, and then tell you how and when they'll purchase it. You need this information to assist them. Therefore, you must use your will to stay focused on achieving that goal.

The *will* sector of the conscious mind also comes into play when setting goals. Have you set your goals for this year? Do you want to be elected to your trade organization? Do you want to be known in your market as, for example, the "expert"—the go-to person people refer their friends to when they want what you offer? It takes will power and determination to achieve your goals, but its well worth the effort.

Intuition—Often referred to as the sixth sense, this vital part of the conscious mind gives you the ability to pick up information in a way that modern science may not be able to explain. Experienced salespeople use intuition to discern their prospects' needs and wants. Owners or managers often use intuition to bring in the correct inventory.

Please understand that *this is a real ability* that you can use consciously. Unfortunately, the part of the conscious mind called *reason* often interferes in making full, confident use of this valuable gift.

MEMORY—Psychologists say that each person has a perfect memory, that nothing gets forgotten. But although your memory is perfect, you may need training to retrieve it through your conscious mind.

Give your memory a bit of help. Far too many salespeople store details in their minds instead of writing them down. That's why you see experienced salespeople taking notes during a conversation with a prospect—and using them during the close or consummation session of a sale. Beware of having a memory of convenience. Our memory can play tricks on us, and even the best professional speakers or television commentators use notes to help them. When it's time to consummate the sale, you have to know the benefits and advantages that are important to the prospective buyer. Too many salespeople try to close a sale, forgetting what the prospective buyer told them was important. Sell them *their* dreams, not yours.

An associate once told me that if you write your goals for next year, put them in a box, and don't even look at them; you'll still accomplish at least 80 percent of them. Why? Because you had to think before you wrote them down and during that thinking process you stored that information in your memory.

Based on that alone, I suggest you write down your complete sales presentation, rehearse it, and safely store that information in your memory. Memorizing your own presentation greatly differs from trying to remember a "canned" sales presentation that someone else wrote for you.

Perception—You can develop your ability to view the world differently than others. You can decide how circumstances will affect your life, and you can learn to perceive and react to your realities in better ways.

Use your Conscious Mind to Stop Negative Thinking.

Suppose you came home one afternoon and found your front lawn littered with garbage. You'd probably be upset, but you'd clean it up right away. Now, think of all the garbage that's littered on the biggest front yard in your world—your mind. You'll recognize this garbage as *negative thinking.* It's all too easy to allow both yourself and others to pollute your mind.

Don't allow that dumping to happen. Don't refuse to do something about it. Put a guard watching the front lawn of your mind—a guard called *reason.* Let your reasoning power kick in to accept or reject ideas. Today's business environment of "making the sale at any cost" requires you to have your guard up all the time. To do that, picture yourself in a positive light. It's great to meet your customers at church or at the mall and have them introduce you to their friends as "the salesperson who found me a great value" rather than "the guy who sold me something." Strive to accomplish that feeling of personalized service with every sale you make.

TAP INTO THE TREMENDOUS CAPABILITY
OF YOUR CONSCIOUS MIND.

Understand the Role of Your Subconscious Mind

The *reason*, *imagination*, *will*, *intuition*, *memory*, and *perception* sectors of your conscious mind work together to make you what you are today. Develop and use all of these. In today's competitive environment, you can hardly do otherwise.

Your subconscious mind, however, is also magnificent. And it's certainly complex, for it's at the center of both your personality and "who you are" as a person. Remember, every thought your conscious mind *chooses* to accept, the subconscious must *willingly* accept, for it has no ability to reject conscious thought.

Because of its complexity (and because I don't have an advanced degree in psychology), I won't go any deeper into the subconscious mind except to state this basic truth: *For every idea that your conscious mind conceives, your subconscious mind will create whatever is necessary to fulfill that picture.*

That means if you carry around pictures of failure in your mind—if you believe that you can't get that loan approved or that a prospect won't buy—your subconscious mind creates exactly that in reality—*failure right on schedule.* All conditioning you've received from your parents, teachers, and authority figures is also housed in your subconscious mind (I suggest reading a great book called, *As a Man Thinketh*, by James Allen to help you better understand this phenomenon).

Whatever is impressed into your personality gets expressed through your actions, including the way you relate to other people, your perceptions, and your work habits. Knowing that, I encourage you to make your subconscious mind work for you.

THE SUBCONSCIOUS MIND MUST ACCEPT EVERY THOUGHT THE CONSCIOUS MIND MAKES.

"Seek out that particular mental attribute which makes you feel most deeply and vitally alive, along with which comes the inner voice which says, 'This is the real me,' and when you have found that attitude, follow it."

—William James

Chapter 9

Set and Achieve Your Goals

All successful salespeople know that to achieve the changes and growth they want, they must identify priorities, set specific goals, and focus resources to achieve these goals. I believe the secret to realizing personal success is to set goals and develop plans a year at a time. When you do, you can deal with the concerns that really matter and make the changes you need to make.

By the age of eight or ten, you probably had an idea of what you wanted in life. You formed a picture in your mind about a possible career and family. As you moved through your teenage years, these goals become even more defined. When you reached your twenties or thirties, you had achieved many of your previous goals while allowing new goals to form.

As life went on in your forties, however, something happened to this logical and valuable process. Goal setting started to become more casual and far less specific. Almost before you realized it, more wants and desires planted themselves in your mind. As an adult, you stopped thinking about goals and followed your nose—simply reacting to circumstances to meet immediate needs rather than planning for the future. As time went by, you felt that your life was spinning out of control; there was nothing you could do.

What Happens When You've Lost Control

Unfortunately, you don't have to be in your thirties or forties for a feeling of loss, frustration, and desperation to envelop you. It can occur at any age. Things still have to get done; you feel you have no choice about doing them. By the time you're finished, you're too tired to think about anything else. You give up on your belief in your ability to make things happen. *You become reactive instead of proactive.*

What happens when you set a goal, start to take action, and then let your drive fizzle? Unfortunately, you may have set important goals *but don't actually believe they can be achieved.* Before long, you've lost your momentum. You've forgotten what you've accomplished and you've forgotten what you do well. As a result, you stop building confidence in yourself and in your ability to succeed. Adding to your dwindling self-confidence, you remember failures while forgetting successes. You lower your sights and lessen your opinion of yourself, becoming frozen in the shadow of your biggest problems. You can't face them.

Yet, part of you won't settle for this—the part that wakes up in the middle of the night contemplating things that matter most. You ask, "What am I doing? What have I really accomplished? When is it going to be my turn? How can I start achieving the things that I should be achieving?"

Perhaps you look at how successful people run their lives and discover a basic truth: Successful people aren't successful because they're always on track. They're successful because they know how to *get back on track.* They know how to refocus, no matter how far off course they might get.

If you feel out of control, here are three ways you can get back on track:

1. Accept that you're not alone.

    Understand and accept that you alone are responsible for staying on course, for defining and moving toward your goals. Accepting this responsibility, however, doesn't mean you have to run your life alone. You can turn to numerous resources—with your greatest resource being other people. That means whatever effort you make on your own, you can multiply it by enlisting the help of others. And they have an extremely valuable resource you don't have: a different point of view. By enlisting other people in your cause, their resources also become your resources.

2. Reclaim your dreams.

The longer you put up with painful situations and don't reclaim your dreams, the more you become diminished in your own eyes and the more you lose your ability to make meaningful changes. You attempt to rationalize your situation by saying, "That's just the way it is!"

If you're in one of these self-defeating situations, you may need to go back into your past. Way back! Remember how many times a baby tries to take a first step before giving up? A baby doesn't know how to give up. A baby doesn't know the difference between success and failure. A baby keeps going until he or she can walk! What if you had the same approach to your life and to your selling? Wouldn't that make a difference?

3. Take that first step!

While ideas can be invaluable to you, nothing happens unless you take your first step. Figure out what you want. That's where everything starts. Take that step and let everything else fall in place.

To chart your course, make a list of what you have to do and learn and whom you need to meet to accomplish your goals. Next, prioritize your list in order of what comes first. Whenever you find a step that is so large it intimidates you, break it down into small, less-daunting steps. Remember, all big problems—all complicated steps or processes—are merely combinations of many small processes.

The result? You have a complete plan of all the steps you need to take to get from where you are to where you want to be. To move forward, your plans and goals have to frighten you or they are too small. Review your goals and action plan daily. If you maintain the right attitude, you can—and will—achieve your goals. Welcome to your successful future!

REVIEW YOUR GOALS AND ACTION PLAN DAILY.

Recognize the Emotions Behind Higher Goals

Goal setting is a process driven by a deep emotional need to succeed—a need to want to earn more, have more, or be more. It's usually driven by the hope of gain or the fear of pain.

Goal clarity equals the ability to both define and reach higher goals. As you begin working on your goals, a natural resistance to change sets in—a resistance that can make you settle for the same established, safe, and secure goals you've always had. Sure, it's easier to keep the status quo, to not rock the boat, to not leave your comfort zone. So you settle for what you've always settled for and nothing changes.

During my sales seminars, I ask, "How much money did you make last year versus the year before?" It amazes me how many people make the same amount each year. *They are limited by a self-imposed level of income!*

You can be kept from reaching your goals by self-limiting thoughts, but the moment you set higher goals, you trigger many emotions, usually in the following order:

> INITIAL EXCITEMENT—The thrill of new possibilities can be intoxicating until you realize how much extra effort is required before change can take place.
>
> DOUBT—You focus on the difficulties or roadblocks. You wonder whether you can overcome them.
>
> CONFLICT—You start to wonder, "Can I actually achieve this new goal? What if I try and fail?"
>
> RESISTANCE TO CHANGE—You become uncomfortable with the idea of changing your habits, beliefs, and routines.
>
> REALIZATION—You realize and internalize the truth of the statement "unless something changes, it will remain the same."
>
> ACCEPTANCE—You achieve a deep belief that you are capable of reaching your new goals.

COMMITMENT—You develop a renewed sense of dedication to whatever work, learning, or effort it might take to reach your new goals.

People who successfully reach their goals almost always experience these seven emotional stages. Unfortunately, far too many people get stalled in the second, third, or fourth stage and progress no further. Then, to prevent any further pain of failure, they unconsciously quit setting goals. They opt to stay where they are and remain at that comfort level.

Make no mistake about it, stages two to four (Doubt, Conflict, Resistance to Change) are formidable emotional barriers—*ones you must move through before you can fulfill your dreams.* Goal achievement is largely an emotional or self-esteem issue; you can only reach the goals that your self-beliefs allow you to achieve. The real challenge, therefore, lies in enlarging your internal picture of what you're *capable of achieving* and what you *deserve to have.*

ENLARGE THE INNER PICTURE OF
WHAT YOU BELIEVE YOU CAN ACHIEVE.

Address the Deeper Issue of Inner Congruence

Reaching goals is not just a matter of knowing how; it's a much deeper issue. Experiencing these typical inner conflicts can significantly limit your performance:

- Setting a goal that conflicts with your basic values.

- Setting a goal that you don't really believe is within your possibilities.
- Living a negative environment (including friends, family, or associates) that keeps you discouraged and emotionally fragmented.
- Not truly believing that higher goals are possible, thereby causing low energy and a little sense of achievement.

Until you work through these conflicts, you'll put forth little effort toward reaching your goals. Conversely, once you build an inner belief that (1) your goals are possible, (2) you deserve to have them, (3) your goals are congruent with your values, and (4) you have a good support system, *you automatically release new energy and a drive to achieve.*

WORK THROUGH YOUR DEEPEST CONFLICTS
AND RELEASE A DRIVE TO SUCCEED.

Release Your Drive to Achieve

You'll find your drive to achieve continually increases as you strengthen your belief that you're capable of reaching your goals—that you deserve the benefits and rewards they'll bring you. This is what separates you from so many others!

If, on the other hand, you believe either consciously or subconsciously that you don't deserve to enjoy higher goals, you'll find subtle, unconscious ways to prove they're impossible to achieve. You'll sabotage yourself and never consciously know it!

Without a strong desire to achieve, however, people may set goals, but *will not* attain them. On the other hand, as your achievement desire gets released, it will multiply your skills, knowledge, abilities, experience, education, and training. This is why if a new prospect approaches you soon after you just closed a sale, you'll probably close that next sale as well. If you have just lost a sale, however, chances are good that you'll also lose the next one. You can break this negative cycle by simply taking a break, walking around the block, thinking positive thoughts, and aiming to regain your confidence.

Have you ever watched the television show *Jeopardy*? Once a person has given a wrong answer, it usually takes two or three more questions before the contestant will buzz in again. But when the person is on a roll, he or she will keep buzzing in. Selling is similar in that when you're selling and above quota, it's easier for you to keep on selling. When you hit a sales slump, the best thing that you can do is take a brief break, regroup your thoughts, and then go back to selling. You'll sell yourself out of the slump. Yes, we've all been there.

Knowing this also helps explain how people with equal knowledge, skill, experience, and education/training can perform on entirely different levels. Do you see how a high achievement drive or desire multiplies the net effect of all our other skills, abilities, and resources?

It's important to understand that an achievement—desire—doesn't get released just because you know about it. Rather, it's the result of having goal clarity and in believing that the goals you've set for yourself are within your possibilities.

You can increase your own achievement desire by practicing positive and/or possibility thinking. I suggest reading as many books as you can on the subject. Rev. Dr. Robert Schuller, Senior Pastor of the Crystal Cathedral has written numerous outstanding books on possibility thinking. The mission statement of the Crystal Cathedral is: "Find a need and fill it. Find a hurt and heal it." This is the type of attitude that a professional sales person should have toward their prospective buyers. When driving, listen to motivational tapes and CDs. Keep your mind in a strong "I can make it happen" attitude. Do all this and great things will happen.

DON'T BE SURPRISED WHEN SUCCESS
BECOMES YOUR CONSTANT COMPANION.

How to Set Effective Goals

Few things in your business or personal life can help you more than setting goals and working toward them. It's a process that, if used correctly, will focus your efforts and give you direction. Achieving your goals acts as a positive self-motivator for everything you do in life.

The basic process is straightforward:

- Determine what you want out of your business and/or personal life.

- Determine what objectives or steps you need to achieve to reach this ultimate goal.
- Determine when you want/need to achieve these steps or objectives that lead to your personal vision of success.

Get prepared to move out of your comfort zone and put some zip into your dreams. If you have a standard goal such as "To Be the Top Sales Person for the Company," that's not good enough. Dream bigger! Set a goal such as "To Be the Top Sales Maker for Your Industry" or "To Set New Company Sales Records."

Use the following process to set goals that will help you do just that:

1. Make your goals your own.

    While this may sound obvious, a far too common mistake is to allow your goals to be designed by someone else. To prevent this, start by asking yourself such questions as, "What do I really want? Do I want to sell cars, floor covering, remodeling, loans, etc.? Do I want to pursue another line of work? What do I really want to do with my life?" Here's the point: When you let other people determine your definition of success, you can sabotage your own future. *This is your life; the goals you set belong to you!*

2. Make your goals meaningful.

    When you prepare to write down your goals, ask yourself these questions: "What's really important to me? What's the purpose of doing this? What am I prepared to give up to make this happen?" While I believe that a career in sales is exciting and profitable, it's certainly not the only path to personal and financial success.

    In addition, ask yourself, "What are the rewards and benefits of my current profession?" Focus on the exciting new lifestyle you can enjoy by committing yourself to dreaming, backed by consistent action.

3. Make your goals specific, have time constraints, and be measurable.

    Here's where most people lose it—by not making goals specific, measurable, and time-specified. Define what you want to accomplish (specific), by when (time constraints), and how you'll know when your goal has been reached (measurable). If you can't measure it, you can't manage it.

4. Make your goals flexible.

    You don't want to design a system that's so rigid you feel suffocated. Yes it should be specific, but not stifling. In addition, a flexible plan allows you the freedom to change course if a genuine opportunity comes along. A word of caution: Being flexible doesn't mean you start chasing every idea that arises and/or use this as an excuse to change your goals.

5. Make your goals challenging and exciting.

When you set goals that you sincerely feel are exciting and challenging, you acquire an edge that prevents you from settling into boredom. To do this, though, you must force yourself to jump out of your comfort zone. It's scary, but that's how you can really grow.

When I was considering moving to a new organization the following poem helped me make the leap. It goes like this:

I used to have a comfort zone
Where I knew I couldn't fail,
The same four walls of busy work
Were really more like jail.

I longed so much to do the things
I'd never done before,
And I stayed inside my comfort zone
And paced the same old floor.

I said it didn't matter,
That I wasn't doing much;
I said I didn't care for things
Like dreams, goals and such.

I claimed to be so busy
With the things inside my zone,

But deep inside I longed for
Something special of my own.

I couldn't let my life go by,
Just watching others win,
I held my breath and stepped outside
And let the change begin.

I took a step and with new strength
I'd never felt before,
I kissed my comfort zone "good bye"
And closed and locked the door.

If you are in a comfort zone
Afraid to venture out;
Remember that all winners were
At one time filled with doubt.

6. Make your goals realistic.

   You may think this contradicts setting goals that are challenging and exciting. A measure of reality, however, helps ensure that you get better results. Most people are unrealistic about their goals when determining the amount of time it will take to achieve them. Perhaps this sentence says it best: "There are no such things as unrealistic goals, only unrealistic time frames."

7. Make your goals align with your values.

   The words "synergy" and "flow" describe any process

that moves effortlessly toward completion. When your goals are in sync with your core values, you set the mechanism for this harmony in motion. And what are your core values? They're anything you feel strongly about that resonates at a deep level of your being.

8. Make sure your goals are in balance with your life.

If you had to live your life over again, what would you do differently? How about spending more time with your family? Playing a new sport? Finding time to travel? When setting your goals, plan time to relax. Remember, professional selling is a time-demanding career. If you're not cautious, it can also lead to burnout and ill health.

9. Make sure your goals include contribution.

A well-known Bible verse says, "Whatever a man sows, that he will also reap" (Galatians 6:7). This fundamental truth implies that if you hand out good things and consistently sow well, you'll receive rewards. Turning this thought to sales, it can also mean that if you constantly prospect for new customers, take care of the ones you have, and get referrals, you'll receive rewards.

10. Find support for your goals.

This particular aspect of goal setting is somewhat controversial. Consider these three points of view:

1. Tell the whole world about your goals and time lines. This makes you accountable, for it's hard to back down when others are watching to see if you'll really do what you said. While there is a lot of pressure when you choose this strategy, certain individuals thrive on it.
2. Set your goals, keep them to yourself, and get on with the job. Actions speak louder than words, and your actions may surprise a lot of people.
3. Selectively share your dreams with a few people you trust—carefully chosen, proactive individuals who will support and encourage you when the going gets tough.

Note: If you chose this third option (probably the wisest of the three), I recommend you only share your goal(s) with people who won't feel threatened by them. It may not, for example, be prudent to tell your sales manager that you plan to have his or her job within a year. A better approach may be to publicly state that your goal is to be the top salesperson. Not only is that goal non-threatening, but your sales manager will probably help you achieve it.

GOAL SETTING REQUIRES YOUR TIME, EFFORT, AND DISCIPLINE—BUT THE REWARDS ARE WORTH IT.

"My own experience has taught me this: If you wait for the perfect moment when all is safe and assured it may never arrive. Mountains will not be climbed, races won, or lasting happiness achieved."

—Maurice Chevalier

Chapter 10

Rely on Marketing and Prospecting, Not Hope

The hoping days are over! I remember when business was booming. We could sit in our office hoping that a prospective buyer with a down payment, good credit, and a desire for our product or service would stop in our office. And it would happen!

But those days are gone. If you plan on staying in business today, you can't rely on hoping that buyers will walk in the door or contact you. Instead, you must take a proactive stance toward growing or, in some cases, maintaining your sales and profits by engaging in actions that bring in sales.

Observing the debris field known as the U.S. economy, business leaders are being exhorted to slow down, take a deep breath, and pull back. Unfortunately, the false comforts of clichés such as "tend to your garden" or "continue with business as usual" or "everything will be okay once interest rates decrease" will not contribute to your success. *Only sales will do that!*

In fact, believing such clichés can be disastrous. Consider the fate of Montgomery Ward: Its leaders did little to ensure the retailer's survival. The management of Montgomery Ward, the first retail department store did nothing to grow their customer base. They were satisfied with status quo. While other merchants were moving to the suburban malls Montgomery Ward remained in the inner cities. While this was a noble act, it was not a good business decision. IBM sold mainframe computers and thought the PC was a joke; that everything would return to business as usual after about ten people bought a computer. Michael Dell thought that everybody should have a computer, both at work and at home. Today, Dell is the largest supplier of computers. Businesses simply won't grow or survive when negative thinking is present.

Get Out, Get Known, and Get Vocal

Because of population growth alone, any market you're in is probably larger than you believed it was. Don't impose limits. Instead, do some soul-searching and answer these two critical questions:

1. Are you out marketing yourself and your product/ service?

2. Are you prospecting for new buyers every day?

If you answered "no" to either question, change it now. Try these ideas:

- Contact your local television and radio stations to be a guest on one of their local talk shows.
- Call your local professional association(s) to discuss how you can have your products on display at their meetings as well as make a presentation.
- Become a featured speaker at local civic clubs or chamber of commerce to tout the advantages of your product or service.
- Support a politician or lobbying group that under stands the needs and benefits of your product or ser vice because a politician can assist you in acquiring major government contracts. A lobbyist can put your company in touch with major corporations that you would not gain access to easily.

- Review your Web site. Many of today's buyers are searching the Internet before venturing out or inviting prospective sellers to visit them.

Continually Prospect for New Buyers

A salesperson that does not have an active prospective buyer's list is out of business—period. Professional appearance, impressive presentations, and superior closing skills just aren't enough to prevent failure. You must have people to whom you can tell your story—and who have both the desire and the ability to buy. Mastering the basics of prospecting is a critical step in the sales process. Without this skill, you can never achieve the success you truly deserve.

To help you achieve that success, I suggest you avoid embracing the five sales myths that surround the critical function of prospecting. They are:

1. First myth: Prospecting is the same as sales.

    While closely linked to sales, prospecting is a separate and distinct function. The job of prospecting is to find qualified leads (people who might [The word "may" primarily indicates permission; you can use "may" but personally I prefer the word "might."] buy your product or service) while discarding any unqualified leads.

2. Second myth: Prospecting is a numbers game.

    The old school of sales prospecting relies heavily on reaching out to a large number of cold (totally unknown to you) contacts. Quality, however, always supersedes quantity. Sales success comes from finding prospects that have both a propensity to buy as well as the means.

    Consider the large financial powerhouses that provided their sales reps with contact lists of people to sell their mortgage and investments products to. Unfortunately, most of these prospects lived in low-income areas and were highly unlikely to buy *any* financial product—they couldn't afford to!

3. Third myth: Scripts are for sales amateurs.

    Many salespeople insist on prospecting without using a pre-written script. Scripting, however, provides the framework of a successful prospecting campaign because it allows you to test the benefits and ask qualifying questions. Be sure to personalize any script so your presentation never sounds "canned."

4. Fourth myth: Prospecting takes time.

    False! Prospecting takes only a few minutes to determine if the lead wants and can afford your product or service. Don't waste time on people who are unmotivated or unable to buy. Remember. Focus on quality, not on quantity.

5. Fifth myth: Close them on the appointment.

Far too many sales reps focus on setting an appointment (e.g., "Would Friday morning or afternoon be better for you?"), then feel disappointed when only 20 percent of those who made appointments show up. What went wrong? The truth is that many prospects find it easier to agree to an appointment than to say they aren't interested. Also, you've set up a situation that's out of sequence. If prospects are remotely interested, send them informational packages first. This allows them to build an interest and lets you turn the lead from warm to hot. It also gives you a logical reason to call back. And when you do call back, your goal is to set the appointment at a time when they're more receptive to buying.

TO HAVE THE SALES SUCCESS YOU DESERVE, PROACTIVELY MARKET AND PROSPECT.

"Alps? No, it's our sales."
"It is time to call Henry."

"All that is necessary to break the spell of inertia and frustration is this: Act as if it were impossible to fail. That is the talisman, the formula, the command of right-about-face that turns us from failure to success."

—Dorothea Brande

Chapter 11
What It Takes to Sell in Difficult Times

With all the changes happening in technology and society today, great salespeople don't sit around wondering, "What's happening?" Instead, they think of innovative ways to create both value and new opportunities for their prospects. During tough times, prospects having good credit, little or no personal debt, and know what they want don't just walk in with checkbook in hand. You have to find them!

While recognizing the anxiety in the air, dig deep into your imagination and create a reason for quality prospects to contact you. Know that they've done their Internet research, read industry papers, and watched economic forecasts on television. They're demanding, informed, and aware that they're a rare commodity—after all, every salesperson seeks this type of prospect.

During my seminars, I explain that today's salespeople must work harder and smarter than ever. All too often, though, I hear the old axiom, "I have to have balance in my life." In hard economic times, my response is this: "If your work life isn't out of balance, your checkbook soon will be." This is exactly the time to work harder and smarter than ever.

Unfortunately, many companies curtail training when budgets are tight. *That's a big mistake!* Granted, this may not be the best time to take staff on a golf outing to Palm Beach with a two-hour conference stuck in the schedule somewhere. But training is essential, especially if you focus on selling strategies during a recession. Training that is time/cost-effective, results-oriented, and specifically focused on increasing sales and profits is invaluable. More than that, it positively affects the attitudes of the sales staff.

The Role of Management: More Critical Than Ever

During tight economic times, sales managers must be present, involved, and loyal to their sales staff. Their task is to inspire their salespeople to go the extra mile because they want to—not because they're afraid of losing their jobs. Salespeople can't sell effectively if they don't have the support of management. *Pump 'em up!*

How can managers keep their sales staff eager to work (and not feeling anxious)? Try the following tactics:

1. Ease off a bit.

   Now is not the time to be a pile driver and a numbers cruncher. The sales staff may need extra managerial attention in downturns, but not the critical, nitpicking kind. In fact, the staff should back off a little. Ironically, the more you need the sale, the more you need to tone down the sale pitch. *Nobody wants to buy from a desperate salesperson.*

2. Be visible.

   It's absolutely critical that managers stay "front and center" in a crisis. By showing your staff that you're calm and committed, you can produce a trickle-down effect that goes like this: managers reassure their salespeople who in turn reassure their prospects.

3. Provide needed training.

As a sales manager, realize that you need trained salespeople to work with the new breed of prospects who will contact you. In addition, the increased amount of documentation required by the new Patriot Act will keep everyone busy just to get the deals funded (To find more information on the Patriot Act, talk with your banker or visit www.USAPatriotAct.com).

4. Talk to your staff.

A good manager lets people vent—complaining about their fears and sales they've just lost. If staff members get discouraged, listen, talk about, and understand their feelings. Make it a point to address all their concerns and questions.

But talking is just part of the solution. While it's vital for people to feel that you hear and understand their concerns, it's even more important that actions be taken. Make it a point to focus on those elements of the situation they *can* control, not the ones they can't. If you've handled this situation correctly, your sales staff should walk out of your office both energized and focused on a plan of action.

5. Set realistic goals.

Nothing is less motivating than shooting for a sales goal that's impossible to reach. In fact, take time to revisit the goals you set during good economic times. I suggest setting goals every month so you can quickly react to changing economic conditions.

6. Teach staff salespeople to vary their selling approach.

   During tough economic times, it's vitally important that staff members relate to their prospects as whole human beings; that they demonstrate they not only understand their needs, but they're willing to work with them on reaching their dreams. Teach salespeople to encourage their prospects to relate to them as trusted advisors, *not as salespeople hungry for commissions.* Ensure they understand that if they're successful in creating this trust, it will pay additional benefits by generating referrals.

During hard economic times, prospects are naturally nervous, so they may delay making purchasing decisions. They need more direction and guidance than they did when money was more plentiful. If there were ever a time when lunging for the quick close might backfire, it's now.

When prospects have objections, a good salesperson concedes to their points, asks them to elaborate, and remains neutral while they talk. They may think they're telling you why they can't or won't buy, but they're really explaining what they need to make the decision. Once you have that information, draw a direct correlation between the features and benefits of your product or service and the advantage of buying from you. Use reassuring language such as, "Its one less thing you have to worry about."

ON-GOING TRAINING IS ESSENTIAL TO KEEP SALES STAFF MORALE HIGH.

'Tis the Season to be Jolly (or Not!)

Conventional wisdom says that the holiday season is a bad time to sell big-ticket items. Sales slow down because people are only thinking about holiday purchases. Given that, maybe you should take a three-month vacation. Right? *Wrong! Wrong! Wrong!*

If this is the way you think, then your sales certainly *will* slow down. Stop thinking you can't sell high-priced products during the winter months and certainly not during the holidays. *Selling isn't a seasonal occupation!* Statistics show that December is a great month to sell houses, autos, and other high-ticket items. I suggest adopting the AAA method of sales and marketing, otherwise known as changing your Attitude, your Action, and your Advertising. Let's look at each of these more closely.

1. Consider your prospects' Attitude.

   What usually happens at the end of the year?

   a. Prospects receive their holiday and end-of-year bonuses—money they can use for a down payment. They're already in the mood for buying.

   b. Children are out of school for an extended period of time, so they're ready to go back to school after the break.

   c. People are buying gifts for others and sporting an "I want to buy" attitude. Capitalize on all of these and use them to your selling advantage.

The winter holiday season is when most retailers traditionally gear up for their largest number of sales. Why not expect the same in other areas of sales? Remember the cliché: *You usually get what you expect.*

Actually, there are many reasons for prospects to buy homes, boats, or automobiles during the months of December to March. Use your imagination and change *your* attitude about *their* attitudes. Think how wonderful it would be if everybody lived in an energy-efficient home, drove a new automobile with the latest technology, or had the time to help design and/or order a new boat or yacht; *and you made it possible.*

Also during the winter months, most financial organizations look for deals to reach their monthly quotas. Now, I'm not suggesting you sell to prospects having bad credit, but the reality is that during this time, lenders will go for marginal deals.

Realize that to be successful in sales, as noted earlier, you have to change your conscious mindset. Remember the old axiom: "If you don't believe that the prospects will buy, they won't." Lack and limitation can exist only when you make room for them in your mind.

Do not forget that everything you have or do is preceded by an image in your mind. Therefore, program your mind to think positively about selling products or services during the winter months.

2. Take Action. You still have to listen, assist, and ask for the order.

Even though the winter holidays may be a season of miracles, you still have to ask for the order! And what about listening? Don't be in a hurry. Listen to your prospects with empathy. Assist them in making the decisions they want to make. Help them determine the best choice for them. Encourage them to buy today and not wait for spring.

Experienced salespeople use their intuition to discern a prospect's needs and wants. You'll be surprised how many unexpected selling situations occur when you keep your eyes, ears, and attitudes open.

And let's not forget prospecting during the holiday months! Are you calling prospects who have visited you before? Keep looking for reasons to make sales. Keep laying the groundwork for people to buy from you, possibly using tax refunds as their down payments. Always put into practice the basics of good selling.

3. Increase, don't decrease, your Advertising.

Those who sell high-ticket items can put themselves out of business thinking that everybody has bad credit, lacks funds for a down payment, or both. Remember a universally accepted principle of advertising: You'll attract the people to whom you advertise. So if your advertisements say: *Low down payment, lowest price in town, or we get everybody qual-*

ified, you'll probably get exactly that—a prospect who can't qualify for your product or service in today's market.

Contrast this with advertising that depicts the ambiance of your office or organization, your positive attitude and the benefits of "buying from me today!" How about increasing your advertising spending during this period instead of thinking about taking a month off?

Get creative. Decide what you have to do to make the winter holiday season a selling season. Let your mind expand. Make this the most profitable one ever. Remember, the average salesperson *lets* things happen; the professional salesperson *makes* things happen.

LAY YOUR PLANS FOR SUCCESS AND USE THE AAA APPROACH TO SALES AND MARKETING.

How to Overcome a Sales Slump

During my seminars, I often hear salespeople talking about the economy and how it adversely affects their selling cycle. While I don't deny that economic fluctuations can affect sales, I also know that most salespeople have an occasional sales slump that *rarely* relates to the economy.

Therefore, what's the problem? As with most investigative approaches, you first define the problem, then you identify and correct the causative factors. As a way to identify these areas, let me suggest two different approaches: one objective or rational and one involving emotions.

1. Take an objective approach.

Define the problem—in this case, a sales slump is "a period of reduced sales regardless of its nature or length." Using the objective approach, the next step is to look at each of the five critical elements in the sales process, identify those factors that are either weak or non-existent, and take corrective action. For example:

1) Are you prospecting?

If not, why not? Do you have a pipeline of well-qualified prospects at all times? If not, that's a problem, and it needs to be rapidly corrected. *Sales won't happen if you don't have customers!*

2) Have you evaluated your attitude?

Attitude is so critical that many sales trainers hold that *all external conditions are the result of attitudes.* Prospects can, and do, pick up on your attitude toward them. And it clearly has an effect—positive or negative—on the sales outcome.

3) Have you rehearsed your sales presentation and included benefits?

Note that I did *not* ask if you have product knowledge. Although knowing your product is vital, people don't buy the product for the sake of the product itself; *they buy what the product will do for them.*

4) Are you listening and understanding what prospects are telling you?

One way to show somebody that you're listening is to take notes. This also helps you discover and respond to any sales resistance you may be getting from the prospect.

5) Are you able to bring the selling process to a satisfac tory conclusion or closing?

Closing is where the top 10 percent of salespeople excel. All prospects have some degree of buyer's resistance and look for reasons not to buy today. It's necessary that you help them focus on both the reason(s) they came to see you and your product or service.

To be a consistent long-term winner, you have to effectively manage all five of these selling stages. *It does little good for you to have great closing skills if you don't have prospects in front of you.*

In short, if you're experiencing a slump, don't look for someone to blame. Instead, manage yourself by asking, "What skills am I lacking or not using to the fullest?" And then take corrective action!

2. Take an emotional approach.

What does a prospecting slump feel like? Do you feel lost? Perhaps you have no idea who you should call today. Your pipeline is empty and you can't seem to get started filling it. You spend more time with unqualified prospects than with those who have the ability to buy. You may have fallen into the trap of substituting *activity for results.*

What does an attitude slump feel like? Do you feel stressed or tired? Have you lost your enthusiasm? Would you rather take a vacation than face another prospect's rejection, or worse, another prospect who doesn't have the ability to buy?

How about a sales presentation slump? Do you spend most of your time talking instead of listening? Has your prospect taken control of the presentation? Are you being asked to give the price before you establish value? Are you trying to sell features instead of the benefits that this prospect asked you about? And how does a closing slump feel? Perhaps your prospects bring up a lot of trivial objections. Perhaps they keep bringing up price and other competitors. Maybe you find out you're not appealing to the real decision maker—that you've been trying to close on an outside source that lacks the authority to make a buying decision.

3. What to do once you identify the cause.

By using either or both of these approaches to problem solving, you can and will identify the problem area. But then what? How can you prevent a sales slump, or more important, snap out of one when it happens? Here are some ideas:

1. Maintain a positive attitude. Keep a record of your successes and review them along with your goals, skills, and attitudes. When you feel discouraged, review your recent wins. Look at the sales awards you have on your office wall. *What! You don't have any?* Make one of your goals this year to be the num ber one sales person for your company and win some awards. You'll be amazed how quickly you can reverse a negative feeling by reviewing your successes.

If your company doesn't have a sales-close ratio log, develop one for yourself and apply these three secrets of success:

- If you can measure it, you can manage it.
- If you manage it, you will focus on it.
- If you focus on it, you will accomplish it!

2. Spend at least an hour a day reading sales training books and/or listening to sale training tapes. Selling is a skill, not luck. You can, and will, get better with added training and knowledge.

3. Plan your work on a daily, weekly, and monthly basis. Through planning, you take control of your work life. Nothing is so defeating as feeling out of control like a leaf wafting in the wind.

4. Be ruthlessly honest with yourself. Don't let yourself off the hook when you have failed to follow through on a promise, goal, or objective you have set.

5. When you do succeed—and you will—reward yourself. At the end of each day, review your gains and losses. Congratulate yourself for the gains. Don't beat yourself up if losses outweigh the gains—as long as you're getting better and learning more.

BE HONEST BUT PATIENT WITH YOURSELF—
AND KEEP SELLING.

"When we put people before possessions in our hearts, we are sowing seeds of enduring satisfaction."

—Beverly LaHaye

Chapter 12
How to Sell to Women Buyers

The feminine force has been building for decades, with traditionally male roles now featuring a female face. Examples are as close as:

- Madeline Albright: Authoring global policies
- Condoleeza Rice: Representing the U.S. as Secretary of State
- Martha Stewart: Influencing home, art, design, publishing, and technology

- Oprah Winfrey: Redefining communication to millions of women
- Suze Orman: Making sense—and dollars—in financial circles
- Statistics reinforce this view. Consider these facts:
- 80 percent of all consumer goods sold are purchased, or influenced by, women
- 50 percent of all cars are purchased by women
- 50 percent of all personal computers are purchased by women
- 48 percent of all stock market investors are women

Understand How Women Buy Differently than Men

As reported by Faith Popcorn, a leading trend tracker, women start businesses at twice the rate that men do. In the U.S. today, there are 9.1 million women-owned businesses generating $3.6 billion annually. Women employ 27.5 million people, more than all Fortune 500 companies combined. Clearly, this is a buying group with which we need to reckon. Ms. Popcorn summarizes this change simply by saying, "Women are different…and they have money."

As a result, consider the following tips for marketing products to women:

- This century signals "The Millennium of Women."
- Women make decisions in a circular, exploring process.
- To women, one size does not fit all.

- Never assume the man in a couple is in charge of purchasing decisions.
- Market to multiple facets of her life (see "peripheral vision," next page).
- Make the buying process comfortable for her.
- Understand that women believe the next purchase will improve their lives.
- Streamline the search for products and services with technology.
- Give her options for customizing her purchase.

The pivotal question becomes, "How can we as an industry capture these dollars?" Simple! Do what's been done all along—only smarter and better.

To tap into the feminine buying psychology, make sure you understand the general differences between men and women. For example:

- The buying process for men is linear, cut-to-the-chase. For women it is circular, exploring, and tactile.
- Women make time and take time where big decisions are concerned. They are definite and deliberate in their search.
- During the greeting and qualifying process, women usually make the following statements, "We're just looking" or "I'll know it when I see it." What they are really saying is, "Please allow me to take my time to make a quality purchase."

- And contrary to the popular myth, women are not impulsive!
- Women are born communicators who share their thoughts and feelings readily. Note: I know this to be a fact. I have a beautiful wife and a wonderful daughter who share their thoughts with me often.
- If something is working for women, they tell their friends about it with an almost religious fervor. Put another way, they don't just buy a product, they *join* a product.

CREATE A BUYING ATMOSPHERE THAT
WOMEN WANT TO SHARE WITH THEIR FRIENDS.

Know What Women Really Want

Whatever their ages, whatever their interests, women seem to have one thing in common: They are faster than a speeding bullet when it comes to getting things done. They are the original multi-taskers (especially if their name is "Mom") and they often hold employment out of the house. To them, being efficient is critical Monday through Friday. On weekends, however, they need room to relax and a place to cook and entertain. If you were selling cookware, for example, novelty, gourmet-quality pieces would be an essential draw for women buyers.

A new marketing concept called "peripheral vision" fully applies to women buyers. It contends that everything surrounding a woman affects her, which is why certain styles and trends thrive. This concept is reflected in catalogs, television shows, and even Internet shopping.

Yes, this emerging women's market provides a fresh opportunity for salespeople—if you understand it. Not only are women buyers more sophisticated than those of a decade ago, but more than 65,000 catalogs are vying for their attention. Therefore, your product or service must be "catalog-perfect" to capture and keep her attention.

If a golden rule exists in marketing to women, it's this: *Anticipate her questions.* If a woman has to ask questions, she won't bother because, generally, women have been conditioned to verbalize their needs with great reluctance. Therefore, put your energy into product or service designs that both surprise and delight her. Specifically, ask for her opinion during the presentation process, and then listen intently. Get her to verbalize her concept of the buying process. Does she want to talk quietly and private? Does she prefer that you leave the door open? Find out!

If you focus on having "control" or "power" in the marketing process, you're missing the bigger (and more profitable) picture. Realize that women want to be co-decision makers with the men in their lives. Also realize that everything matters when you're marketing to women buyers. They notice and care about the smallest details. Think twice, and then again, about your product or service, your philosophy, your advertising, your marketing, and your sales environment. Do they appeal to women? If not, it's time for a detailed review of your products/services. To ignore this growing market is a major mistake.

TODAY'S WOMAN BUYER WANTS TO BE RESPECTED, APPRECIATED, NURTURED, AND NOTICED.

"Setting an example is not the main means of influencing others; it is only the means."

—Albert Einstein

Chapter 13
Training: How to Guarantee Results

As a professional trainer for many years, I've seen amazing results from organizational training. Unfortunately, I've also seen training programs fail miserably, wasting time, money, and effort. What makes the difference?

I suggest it's from a failure to accurately define organizational problems and to create the right organizational climate for the newly acquired skills, knowledge, and abilities (SKAs) to be used. A closer look at these factors sheds light on why training is so effective in some organizations, but fails totally in others.

While individual trainers may work from slightly different models, most professional training programs contain the following steps:

1. Define and verify organizational needs.
2. Create an organizational climate that ensures newly acquired SKAs are used.
3. Conduct the training.
4. Integrate, support, and reward the new SKAs.
5. Freeze new behavior and procedures.
6. Provide periodic "refresher" training.
7. Conduct a final evaluation and follow-up.

While the above steps define a logical sequence of events, the critical determinant in a successful training program is managerial support and interaction, starting with accurately defining organizational needs.

Defining Organizational Needs

Because training should respond to either a present or future organizational need, accurately *defining that need is critical.* Sounds simple, doesn't it? Just identify the problem and fix it!

All too often though, the real organizational need neither gets identified nor defined. Don't fall into the expensive trap of hiring training designed to provide staff with the skills, knowledge, and abilities to solve problem "A" when

"B" is the real problem. The results won't be effective. For example, if the real issue is having the wrong product at the wrong price for your market and/or not advertising effectively (all marketing factors), teaching staff how to be better sales representatives probably won't solve this problem.

But accurately identifying organizational need(s) isn't easy or simple. While top management quickly becomes aware of decreases in the bottom line (thus signifying a problem), staff training may not always be the right solution. It depends on the problem.

Therefore, consider taking the following actions:

1. Hire a consultant.

One approach to defining an organizational problem is hiring a knowledgeable consultant to identify the core problems. Bringing in an outside expert is a way to overcome the all too common problem of being unable to objectively observe the situation—"being too close to the forest to see the trees." In other words, we can see issues and/or problems in another's organization (or personal life) that we probably can't see in our own life or organization (If you doubt this, just ask your spouse).

Notice that I suggest hiring a knowledgeable consultant—one who is both mature and skilled in organizational fact-finding. By its nature, organizational fact-finding implies a certain degree of criticism that can be disruptive if it's not handled properly. It takes the right kind of person to establish and maintain a positive climate of acceptance, trust, and confidentiality so that the sales staff can talk freely and honestly about both their individual and work-related problems.

2. Question if training is the best solution.

Once organizational issues and/or problems are accurately identified, it's necessary to question if staff training is the fastest, most cost-effective way to address them. A skilled trainer should be able to explain how training can directly address the defined needs. If a professional trainer is unable to do this, hire someone else.

The decision to conduct training sessions should come only after (1) organizational and staff needs have been accurately identified, (2) a logical tie-in has been made between the content of the proposed training and its ability to address these needs, and (3) there is managerial commitment to use and reinforce the new SKAs provided by the training.

MAKE A LOGICAL TIE-IN BETWEEN IDENTIFIED PROBLEMS AND TRAINING AS A SOLUTION.

Creating the Right Organizational Climate

Even after organizational needs have been accurately identified and training proposals have been analyzed and verified, success won't be assured if the organizational climate isn't right.

While almost any training program will result in participants learning new skills, knowledge, and abilities (SKAs), that's not the issue! Management needs to ensure an organizational commitment to:

- use the newly acquired SKAs,
- integrate the new SKAs into everyday workings, and
- recognize and reward their use.

To help meet these requirements, there needs to be both commitment and support for the planned training among various levels of management. Consider the following "how not to do it" scenario:

> The CEO of a company unilaterally decides to conduct a series of training sessions, either on site or at another location. The CEO doesn't involve the sales managers of the various regions in the decision to train, nor does the CEO discuss why the training is necessary, what it's supposed to accomplish, who should attend this training, or where or when it should be conducted.

Such unilateral actions will almost certainly result in no emotional commitment to the proposed training among the various managers. Remember, commitment to a decision or action comes primarily from participating in the fact-finding and decision process. People rarely feel committed to decisions made by others without their input. But there's more.

The local sales managers are now told that they don't have to attend the training because they need to continue to manage the sales center. The sales managers are also told to schedule their sales staff to attend the training sessions so that the operation of their sales center won't be disrupted. Not only will this approach further ensure that the newly acquired SKAs won't get implemented, but the sales managers may now regard this new training program as a threat.

Members of the sales staff now complete their training and return to their individual centers. But the local sales managers (who didn't attend this training and thus knew little about it) do know that:

- They had no say in the training or whether it was needed,
- They had to work harder because their staff was at training,
- Their sales center's productivity went down because it was undermanned, and
- depending on the commission structure, their

> pay checks probably suffered due to their center's reduced sales volume. Under this scenario, the local sales managers will not only resent the training program, but they may also resent the staff members who attended this training.

The results? Tension between staff and sales manager's increase, morale declines, productivity is down, money has just been wasted on training, and training is deemed ineffective.

Remember, training is an interim process, not an end objective. The true organizational objective is not just to provide staff with new skills, knowledge, and abilities, but also to fully integrate, support, and employ these new SKAs. And this requires a host of supporting factors other than just a properly designed and delivered training program!

SUPPORTING FACTORS MUST BE IN PLACE
FOR TRAINING TO MEET ITS OBJECTIVES.

"Success is knowing the difference between cornering people and getting them in your corner."

—Bill Copeland

Chapter 14

Team Selling: You Never Sell Alone

Team selling is using the full resources of your company, contractors, and suppliers to establish a deep, lasting, and profitable relationship among people, products, and companies.

Certainly, success in selling a complex product or service is the result of clear planning and effective execution. But it also requires the careful coordination of many resources on both the selling and client side—coordination that's required throughout the life of the sale.

Remember, a sales person is one part of an organization or system attempting to succeed financially. It's irrational to think that any one individual could be solely responsible for all aspects of market research, advertising, ordering, warranting the product or service, selling it, financing its sale, installing and servicing it, and training the user. Your goal in team selling is to establish a lasting and profitable relationship with the other individuals/departments that play a role in the sale of your product/service. To achieve this goal, you absolutely need additional resources because both decision-making and support of most complex product or service happens at many levels.

To determine if you need to the capabilities of a team approach, answer these five questions:

- Can a communications breakdown cost you a sale?
- Do you or your sales people make commitments that subcontractors or departments within your organization won't or can't keep?
- Does your competition get and give bids faster than you do?
- Are your competitors funding deals faster than you are?
- Do you hear customer complaints about after the sale training, or quality of the service or product?

If you answered "yes" to any of these questions, team selling might be the answer. The question now is how do you go about implementing a team selling process?

How to Implement a Team Selling Process

First, identify every individual, department, and organization involved with the sale, financing, and service of your product or service. Next, define the roles and responsibilities of each of these individuals/organizations. For example:

> Secretary/Receptionist—Greets customers on the phone or in person and makes them feel welcome. This is one of the most important positions within your company. Their title should, "*Director of First Impressions.*"
>
> Salesperson—Greets and qualifies customers; present the benefits of the product or service; closes or consummates the sale.
>
> Sales Manager—Trains and assists the sales staff in selling and closing the sale.
>
> Finance and Insurance Manager—Obtains credit approval and funds sales.
>
> Service Manager—Provides after-sale service support as defined and promised in the purchase contract at an agreed-upon price.
>
> Supplier/Wholesaler—Delivers the product at the time, place, and cost agreed upon.

Once the critical individuals are identified, establish a meeting with these individuals/ groups to:

- verify the accuracy of the assigned job descriptions,
- discuss and clarify any problems occurring in each area of responsibility, and
- verify that each of these employees or subcontractors have the support they need to do their job.

Include these people in your monthly update meetings. Remember, if there was no previous emphasis on team selling, you may be faced with changing a corporate culture, and that may require numerous meetings. You'll find that the results, however, are well worth the effort.

WITH A COMPLEX PRODUCT/SERVICE,
THERE'S NO ALTERNATIVE TO A TEAM APPROACH.

"Internalize the Golden Rule of sales that says, All things being equal, people will do business with, and refer to, those people they know, like, and trust."

—Bob Burg

Chapter 15
Follow-Up: The Road to Referrals

Consider these two common scenarios:

> *Scenario* #1: A prospective customer comes into a show room, spends time with a salesperson, looks at the product or service, and then walks away, never to be heard from again.

> *Scenario* #2: A salesperson has just made a sale, given himself or herself well-earned accolades, and then, mentally and emotionally, closes the door on that event and goes on to the next sales opportunity.

Sound familiar? They should; these two scenarios are played out hundreds (if not thousands) of times a day in the sales profession. Unfortunately, both are guaranteed to have a negative effect on a salesperson's income and possibly on his or her future as a sales professional.

What's the problem? In the first scenario, the prospect just walked away and was never heard from again; there was nothing else to do. In the second example, after the sale was made, it was both normal and proper to put it aside and go on to the next one. Right?

Wrong!

In both cases, the sales process emotionally and physically stopped. Instead, the process should have signaled the *start* of the follow-up and referral phase, not the *end* of the sales process.

To explain this position, let's look at the following five topics:

1. The need for follow-up
2. How to follow up successfully
3. Organizing your follow-up process
4. Obtaining referrals
5. Learning not to "cross the annoyance" threshold.

Base Follow-Up on Your Prospects' Needs

Let's review a few facts about successful sales:

- A consistent and persistent follow-up has proven to be one of the most important factors in the sales process.
- Having an organized, systematic approach to follow-up while creatively individualizing your methods based on the prospects' needs improves your selling success.

Today's competitive markets demand a variety of aggressive and thorough follow-up methods that even a few years ago would have been considered unnecessary. Now it's essential to follow up with people considered to be marginal inquiries and you can do so with methods such as sending a *thank-you* letter via e-mail.

In today's competitive marketplace, doing a professional follow-up on everybody who comes to your office or invites you to visit theirs is essential. It's also critical that the follow-up happens quickly.

A professional follow-up doesn't begin with, "Hi, this is the salesperson you just spoke with. Have you made a decision yet?" Instead, it offers new information based on those features and benefits they liked about your product. This new information, in effect, requires them to restart the buying process again—and allows you another opportunity to close the sale.

How well do prospects respond to follow-up inquiries? I'm often asked that question and the answer is always the same: *The response to your follow-up depends entirely on the effectiveness and efficiency of the method you use.* For example, misspelling names, addressing the wrong product or service, or calling your prospect during dinner and asking, "Have made a decision yet?" doesn't encourage prospects to revisit you or your product/service. Not surprisingly, the response you get also depends on whether your prospects have both the *ability* and the *desire* to buy.

Don't get discouraged if some prospects don't respond at all. Sometimes no matter how good your follow-up methods are, you get a big "zero." But when you get a "zero" more times than a "yes," consider re-evaluating your follow-up methods.

Knowing which methods work best for you and which types of prospects respond to one method of follow-up compared with another takes both time and diligent record keeping. Be patient. Nobody ever said selling was easy work. Profitable? Yes. Easy? No.

EFFECTIVE FOLLOW-UP TECHNIQUES REQUIRE BOTH CREATIVITY AND EFFORT.

Employ Follow-up Tactics that Create a Need

Your customers will remember you if you offer them a memorable experience. If you see follow-up as a boring, tedious, and repetitive process, then you can expect your prospects to feel the same way—bored and tired by your constant contacts.

Therefore, it's important to create a need in the minds of your prospects. And this need is directly proportionate to the enthusiasm and creativity you put into your follow-up program. Choose from the following methods and make sure that your methods—and the messages you send through them—add up to a rewarding and memorable experience.

1. Make a telephone call.

    A telephone follow-up is perhaps the most common and least expensive method to use. Unfortunately, it's often the most difficult one to turn into a memorable experience. Why? Just look at all the ways your prospects can miss you. They can avoid your calls by using screening devices such as Caller ID. Your prospects may just be busy so that buying your product or service may not be important to them the day you called.

    Whether or not your phone calls are being screened, get creative and instill enough interest in your voicemail messages to make prospects want to talk with you. Prepare messages that get their attention, pique their curiosity, and entice them to call you back. Consider this effective follow-up message: "*After you left our office, I called the manufacturer of that (home auto, boat) you liked and found out that they have a tremendous incentive for new customers. Please call me as soon as possible. Thanks.*"

2. Send an immediate e-mail.

    In addition to using the telephone, also use e-mail. Send a note that says, "Thank you for allowing (name of organization or company) the opportunity to satisfy your ____ needs. After you left, we discussed your needs and my sales manager suggested _______." When they get check their email, they have an immediate message to read rather than one sent later through regular mail. In some cases, your message through the mail may arrive after they've purchased what they need from someone else. Note: When sending an e-mail, always include your telephone number in the message and encourage your prospect to call you.

3. Mail a thank-you note.

    If your prospects don't use e-mail and don't answer the phone, use the postal service. Remember the importance of a thank-you note? Everyone likes to be appreciated, so use your follow-up system to send a handwritten note of appreciation. This method also lets your prospects know you understand their needs and want their business.

Sending a thank-you note is absolutely necessary when you receive a referral. Another time to send a thank-you is on the anniversary dates when customers purchased your product or service. Sincerely thank your customers for allowing you to satisfy their needs and ask them what else you can do for them. You will be pleasantly surprised how many will call you with a referral. And the sales cycle starts all over again.

4. Use a direct mail approach.

   Direct mail is also a common method of follow-up. Unless your mail-out contains the critical personal touch, however, it won't convey the "we care about you and your needs" message that is so essential to a follow-up. If you do use direct mail, personalize each letter or post card by hand addressing each piece. At a minimum, print your customers' names on the envelopes. Don't use labels; they're too impersonal! After all, you're only sending out about twelve to fifteen a day—not a mass mailing.

PERSONALIZE YOUR COMMUNICATIONS—
IT MAKES A HUGE DIFFERENCE.

How to Organize Your Follow-up System

Maximizing results from your activity is a great goal to have in handling any contact, not just a follow-up. To do so, however, requires efficiency, a well-laid plan, and good records. In Chapter Two, "Create the Desire To Buy," I stated that "the notes you take now will be invaluable later." This is one of those later times. Today, these notes allow you to personalize your follow-up and help you close your sales.

To ensure that your follow-up program is effective (and because follow-up is a constant in the selling process), organize your time and program so you maximize your sales efforts.

A follow-up system can be set up in several ways; choose the method that works best for you. For example, use something as simple as customer registration cards to keep track of your prospects. Or use a more sophisticated filing program. In today's world of professional selling, keep your follow-ups on a sales-force automation software program—one designed to store the maximum amount of information in the minimum amount of space. This may prove to be the most efficient system of all. By setting up a database specially designed for follow-up, you save time and energy that you can then devote to face-to-face selling.

Whichever way you choose to organize your time and the follow-up information you collect, your method should let you systematically and periodically keep in touch with all of your contacts, *including your past clients.*

In your communications, be specific. You can let your prospects and customers know your work schedule. They will appreciate being able to reach you when you say you will be available. Keeping your schedule is just another way to let your clients see how efficiently you run your business.

PEOPLE LIKE TO DO BUSINESS WITH AN ORGANIZED SALESPERSON.

Master the Art of Getting Referrals

Referrals are a great source of business that are easy to get, provided you stay in touch with the people who have trusted you to satisfy their needs. In short, stay connected!

But are referrals effective? Absolutely! Studies have shown that experienced professional salespeople spend only half of the time selling a referred, qualified lead that they would spend selling a non-referred, non-qualified lead—*with a much higher closing rate.* Although a referral is not a guaranteed sale, contacting a person who has been referred is definitely easier than calling someone with whom you have no connection.

Sales wisdom says, Avoid *harassing your prospects and customers.* Recognize when keeping in touch with your prospects has crossed the line and becomes a bother. While determining this line is sometimes difficult, you defeat the entire purpose of follow-up if you fail to recognize a sign of annoyance a prospect sends your way. If prospects hang up on you, it's a good bet that you've crossed their annoyance threshold. In short, be sensitive to their needs. Don't call them on a Friday evening or just before a holiday. They don't consider this kind of call as following up; they'd call it an irritation.

See if these ideas can work for you:

- Keep your follow-up calls short, and call at times most convenient for each prospect's schedule. Interruptions are sometimes unavoidable, but always apologize and call later.
- Be polite! Find out when they expect their needs to change and ask permission to follow up at that date.
- Be relaxed. Remember, you're only selling an appoint ment for them to return and continue a conversation that's already started.
- If your prospects admit that they have purchased from your competitor, don't get upset. Ask if you can take up just a few more moments of their time to get their advice on how you can improve your sales skills, prod uct, or service. Always keep learning how to improve your selling skills.

Like other sales techniques, follow-ups and referrals take work, planning, and practice. But first, understand their value in the entire sales process, and then put these techniques into practice.

Zig Ziglar comments, "Selling is the highest paying,

hardest job you can have or the lowest paying easiest job you can have." Which one do you want? We all have to make choices. I can only assume that since you are reading this book, you want to be one of the highest paid. Congratulations!

USE THE FOLLOW-UP/REFERRAL PROCESS TO YOUR FINANCIAL AND CAREER ADVANTAGE.

"Precision of communication is important, more important than ever, in our era of hair-trigger balances, when a false or misunderstood word may create as much disaster as a sudden thoughtless act."

—*James Thurber*

Chapter 16

Trust: The Essential Element in Sales

Creating trust depends on many factors, and one of the most important is behavior. And because your behavior during the selling process is heavily influenced by how you see your role, let's start by talking about the role you take.

Are you familiar with the image of the "lie at any cost just to make the sale" salesperson, no, I will not refer to that person as a sales person. They are what they are–a liar. It's a well-known way of characterizing overly aggressive salespeople. In fact, this is such a common and powerful image that if you're new to sales, you may even questions your ability to sell because you don't see yourself as a pushy, aggressive high pressure type of salesperson.

Do not have any doubts on that matter. I have been extremely successful in sales and I never had to resort to lying to make a sale. As I stated earlier, people absolutely love to buy, even professional buyers. They want to be treated with respect. Yes, they want to buy from a knowledgeable and confident sales person.

When I ask participants in my sales seminars to define their roles, it's not uncommon to hear, "My job is to sell my product and to do whatever it takes to make that sale." Unfortunately, overly aggressive salespeople who say this are seldom successful long term. Most sales trainers agree that no customer wants to be sold! Therefore, selling isn't about convincing people they need to buy what you sell. Instead, *selling is about identifying a need and solving it.* When you accomplish that—with or without an immediate sale—trust follows.

Establish the Right Foundation

But trust is more than just convincing prospects that you're honest. *You must also convince them they won't waste their time or money buying from you.* Remember, in one way or another, every prospective buyer has been burned by a salesperson. That's why you need to work hard to win that trust anew.

As the foundation of every good sale, trust means customers believe in you and respect your knowledge, your customer service department's standards, and your approach to relating to them. Before they will trust you, they need to like *both* you and the way you operate. Here are three ways to accomplish that:

1. Set the right tone.

   To set the right tone, first acknowledge others in your organization that plays a role in the buying and, in some cases, the installation process. You then give an overview of yourself and your company. When you do this, you answer their initial questions (e.g., Who are you? What's your company's mission statement? How long have you been in business? How long will the buying process take?) And you reduce any concerns while coming across as an organized professional.

2. Search in depth for their specific needs.

   Building trust with your prospective buyer requires that you diligently search for their specific needs. Once you've identified those needs, you then explore solutions and gain agreement on how your product or service will satisfy them. *You see, they need to be convinced that you keenly want to help them find a solution, not just sell them something.* Indeed, most prospects are predisposed to assume that you, like so many other salespeople, only want to make a sale, not find out their particular requirements.

3. Focus energy and attention on your prospects.

   As the selling conversation progresses, prospects take in all of the cues. They listen to your tone of voice and watch your body language. To build trust, be sure to stay calm, be centered, be present, and focus all your energy on the prospect. Concentrate on finding common ground. Build rapport by asking questions and by letting your prospects talk.

BEFORE THEY WILL TRUST YOU,
THEY NEED TO LIKE BOTH
YOU AND THE WAY YOU OPERATE.

Take Care When Asking Questions

Beware. While asking questions is essential, it can also be risky. Using the wrong questions can alienate your prospects or even end the sales presentation. Therefore, it's important to think carefully about the questions you want answered. Good questions shouldn't stump or embarrass. Instead, they should encourage your prospects to think more specifically about their requirements, particularly in relation to how your product or service can answer their need(s).

Astute buyers might volunteer the type of information

that will help you, but only if they perceive that it will benefit them. To establish this perception, you might say, "To assist you in selecting a ____ (product or service), it would be helpful to know a little more about you and your needs." Then proceed to ask questions using these five techniques:

1. Layer your questions.

   Sometimes the prospect's first response to your questions is too vague. Dig deeper by asking another question that elaborates on the answer to the previous question.

2. Use closed-ended questions sparingly.

   A closed-ended question generally elicits a simple "yes" or "no" answer. While there are times you need to get specific information, remember that this type of question can stop a conversation. To restart it, follow any closed-ended question with one that's open-ended.

3. Avoid "choice" questions.

   An example of a choice question would be "Do you prefer a gas or diesel engine?" Like closed-ended questions, they usually elicit a short response and can quickly stop the conversation.

4. Move from general to specific questions.

   Start with broad questions and narrow them down as the conversation progresses.

5. Don't explain features until you have explored your prospects' needs in detail.

If they ask about features, explain that you first need information to assist them in the buying process. If they're really interested in buying, they'll appreciate your interest and provide the information you request.

ASK QUESTIONS THAT WILL REVEAL YOUR PROSPECTS' NEEDS QUICKLY.

Facilitate the Sale, Don't Push It

Even customers who *want* to buy like to believe it was their decision to purchase your service or product. Selling, then, is about enabling customers to *sell themselves*. Given that your customer is the true salesperson, you take on the role of a knowledgeable facilitator, helping identify the best solution(s).

If you don't currently see yourself in the role of a knowledgeable facilitator, you might benefit from adjusting your thoughts in the form of affirmation statements. I find these four affirmations to be effective and suggest that you try them.

Customers want to buy.

I am fulfilling my prospective buyer's needs.

My prospective buyers sell themselves.

I'm helping my clients identify the
best solutions for themselves.

TAKE ON THE ROLE OF A KNOWLEDGEABLE FACILITATOR.

If you want to maximize your sales experience, don't push it, but bide your time and size up the consumer.

"Real integrity is doing the right thing, knowing that nobody's going to know whether you did it or not."

—*Oprah Winfrey*

Chapter 17
Relationships: Follow the Laws

Making and maintaining positive relationships is critical in achieving success as a professional salesperson. Why? Because having a good relationship with your prospects, customers, organization, fellow workers, and other team members is important, not only in selling but in living a fulfilling life. Remember, the quality of your relationships with other people determines your success in sales as much or more than any other factor!

As emphasized throughout this book, *customers don't*

buy features. First and foremost, they buy you as a person. If you don't establish a relationship with your prospects, you'll probably never have the opportunity to tell them about either the features of your product/service or the advantages of buying from you and your organization.

To help you succeed in both sales and in your personal life, I suggest you apply these five laws of relationships:

1. First law: Relationships are Essential

   The more people who know you and think of you in a positive way, the more opportunities you'll have to achieve your goals. Now, think this through. "The more people who know you..."—yes, you know a lot of people, but do they really know you? If a prospective customer asked a few of your present customers about you, what would they say? Would they talk about you in a positive way?

   Every important change in your life involves other people, be it a new spouse, a baby or new child, or even a new boss. If you want to achieve big goals, *you need the active involvement and cooperation of other people.* It's possible that your day, and even your entire life, could be changed by a single comment, a piece of advice, or a single action by another person. Chances are the more good relationships you have and the more helpful people you know, the more the doors of opportunity will open for you.

2. Second law: Law of Probabilities

The more different things you try, the more likely you'll try the right thing at the right time.

Stated another way, the more people you know and the more you expand your contacts, the more likely you will meet the person you need to open doors for you.

There is an old saying that when the student is ready, the teacher will appear. In the world of selling, the more prospects and other centers of influence you know on a personal level, the more likely the right opportunity will appear.

Unless you are fortunate enough to have established business connections, you must work at creating and building relationships. A major part of selling is establishing positive relationships with everybody you encounter.

Note: I use the "arm-reach method of relationships." If you are within an arm's reach of me, I start telling you what I do for a living and try to establish if you are a prospect. If not, I'd ask if you know someone who might be. If you use the arm-reach method often enough, you'll connect with people who harmonize with your dominant thoughts. These are the people who will buy from you.

3. Third law: Law of Indirect Effort

You get what you want with other people indirectly rather than directly.

Whoa, you say! Haven't traditional sales trainers told you to "get in their faces and sell, sell, sell." Using an indirect selling method requires that you ask questions, ask questions, and then ask more questions. You take an interest in your prospects by asking questions and listening to what they say. Be empathetic. Express sincere concern about their problems and situations.

Note: This is not the time to tell your prospects you can solve all their problems. Rather, keep establishing a relationship. You'll be amazed at how often they ask if you can help them. By asking questions, the indirect approach establishes a relationship in which the prospect may even ask you to let him or her buy your service or product.

Why does the indirect approach work? You might also ask why people generally dislike salespeople. The answer: Because salespeople have traditionally been taught to "go direct" at their prospects, trying to close the sale at the initial contact without establishing a relationship or showing prospects they care about them as people. The result: most prospects feel they only represent a commission check to you.

One or two interpersonal factors often arise during the sales process: trying to impress others and/or trying to gain their respect. The worst approach is the direct way—by trying to impress them. A far better way is *to be impressed by other people.* Realize that the more impressed you are with other people and their accomplishments, the more interested and impressed they will be with you. I believe that everyone has done something noteworthy and impressive. When you first communicate with a prospect, find out what that is!

Specifically, ask your prospects what they do for a living and how they got into their field of work. Also ask about hobbies and family interests. When a person mentions having achieved something, give out compliments. By using the Law of Indirect Effort, you constantly look for ways to compliment and congratulate people on what they've accomplished, including any positive changes in their lives.

Do you want people to respect you and think of you as an expert in your field? Considering that almost everything a professional salesperson does in their daily selling, requires earning the respect of fellow workers and customers, *this is one of the deepest of all needs.*

However, you can easily accomplish a high level of respect by showing respect to your clients and co-workers in advance. Respect the fact that your prospects worked hard for their money. Respect the fact that your co-workers are valuable members of the team. Respect that your employer has invested in a company that creates an opportunity for you to sell a product/service you believe in.

4. Fourth law: Law of Reciprocity

To receive, you must first give.

Successful people always look for ways to do things for other people. We've left the "go-getter" era of the 1990's, and we now live in the era of the "go-giver." The great majority of underachievers and unhappy people wait for others to do something for them! They want to get something "out" before they put something "in." But according to natural laws, you can't reap a reward without first sowing something. When you establish relationships with others, you are sowing seeds for possible sales and reaping the benefits that a good income brings.

And why does this law of reciprocity work? Simply stated, when you do something nice for another person, it raises your own self-esteem and makes you feel better about yourself. This heightened feeling of positive energy activates your powers of attraction. As a result, you become a powerful magnet for people and circumstances consistent with your goals. Good things start to happen to you. There is something about helping a deserving person have the pleasure of experiencing the product or service you sell and in which you believe.

At times, you may deal with a prospective buyer who has poor credit. This is not necessarily a bad person, just someone who has made bad life decisions. While you can't possibly sell that person your product/service, you can still give him or her something—*your respect.* When people feel respected, they will refer co-workers or family members who have good credit to you resulting in a sale.

Universal law allows for these things to come back to you in the most remarkable ways. *The law is there and it works, so use it!*

To illustrate this law, consider the life of John D. Rockefeller who began working as a clerk earning $3.75 a week. This is not a misprint. For years, he saved 20 percent of his income, gave 50 percent away, and lived on the remaining 30 percent. By the time he reached the age of fifty-two, Rockefeller had become the richest man in the world.

This is to say not to give away your earnings in hopes of a larger return. Here, we have a reverse saying of the popular phrase, "To receive, you must give."

5. Fifth law: Law of Positive Relations

Once you have made some decisions about what you want in your personal life, it's time for you to decide what kind of relationships you want in both your career and personal life.

One of the secrets of a successful work life is to carefully choose both your boss and your company. Remember, you are exchanging your life—you're most valuable possession—for the opportunity to work, to get results, and to obtain the income that comes with success. Your success at work depends on the quality of the relationship you have with your boss, your co-workers, and your customers.

If you think you're working for an unethical boss or company, *quit today!* You'll never be a success there! Many good people have left a negative work environment and joined a different retailer or manufacturer led by a positive, optimistic, encouraging boss, and a group of great co-workers. In no time, a person who was doing poorly in one environment thrives and grows in the new environment. Your choice of mate, friends, organization, boss, and co-workers are important, so build relationships with the "right" people. Spend time with winners; get away from negative people—those who complain, condemn, and criticize. *This demanding profession requires you to surround yourself with positive people.*

SMART PEOPLE REFUSE TO KEEP WORKING IN A NEGATIVE SITUATION.

Ways to Build Successful Relationships

To expand your application in the Laws for Relationships, adopt the following ideas.

1. Select one or two organizations whose members can assist you in achieving your personal and business goals.

   When you've identified a committee to which you can make a valuable contribution, volunteer for that committee. Most people who join associations do little more than attend the meeting and social functions. *They regard the meeting as an extension of their social lives rather than as a critical part of their business lives.*

2. Choose your friends and associates with care.

   Your reference group is made up of the people with whom you identify and associate with most of the time. Associate with people who are experts in your selling career of choice.

3. Side with a-loners.

   This doesn't mean "a-loners" are loners. They have lots of friends, but they don't go out to lunch with whoever is standing by the door at the time. Selective in their relationships, they insist on only spending time with people they enjoy and whose company can benefit them.

4. Get involved in your community.

You'll find there are always vastly more opportunities to serve your community then talented and caring people to fill those slots. You can easily expand your contacts and relationships if you approach each situation as a "giver" rather than a "taker." Why not start today?

BE A "GIVER" RATHER THAN A "TAKER" AND YOU'LL BUILD FULFILLING RELATIONSHIPS.

"Henry's training PAYS OFF."

"The frustrating thing is that the key to success doesn't always fit your ignition."

—*Roger C. Meyer*

Chapter 18

How Customers Buy (Not How You Sell)

Many companies try to improve their sales results by developing or adopting a formal sales process. Unfortunately, not all companies who formalize their sales process realize the results they expect. In fact, most of these processes fail because they're not designed around one simple truth: Most sales professionals only get paid (and meet quotas) based on what prospective buyers do, not on what the salesperson does. They have to sign a contract before you make money. Isn't that the way it works?

Stated another way, companies try to get their salespeople to follow a series of stages, steps, and activities in order to make the sale. What's missing? Simply this: *prospective buyers must work through their own steps in order to buy.* Beware that at any particular step or stage, what you do could be a complete waste of time if your prospect doesn't do what's needed to move forward in the purchasing process.

Prospects Determine the Selling Process, Not You

Earlier chapters addressed interviewing and asking prospective buyer's good questions e.g., first ask about their present situation and then their desire to obtain the type of product or service you sell. They also discussed ways to communicate with prospective buyers during the entire selling process. For example, some companies advocate that once a contract is signed, the prospect should communicate only with the department responsible for implementing the sale. *This is absolutely wrong.* I suspect the people who teach this have never sold a major product/service or failed in their efforts. Remember, people tend to buy based on the salesperson's credibility—not that of your company, the manufacturer of your product, or from any other department within your organization. Therefore, it's *your prospects* who determine how effectively you communicate. Making a sale simply does not depend on a formalized sales sequence. There is another–ABC–rule that, as a sales executive, I have used, Always Be Communicating!

Sales managers tend to encourage their sales staff to ask a question like, "What do we need to do to close this deal?" But that's not the right question, because you could do forty-seven different things and still not get the deal done. The question you should be asking yourself is, "What does the prospective buyer need to do in order to buy?" Only when you've answered that question are you ready to ask this follow-up question: "What do I need to do to get the prospective buyer to take action?"

Rather than simply checking the box next to the steps of your sales process, look at each opportunity in your sales pipeline and ask these four critical questions:

1. What does this particular buying process look like?

    Buying and approval processes vary, but all have one factor in common: communication. Every time you come in contact with a prospective buyer, you have an invisible shield between you and the other person. How you communicate determines if that shield comes down or if it gets thicker. To even begin the buying process, you must make that shield disappear. In real estate sales, for example, instead of saying, "This is the kitchen," say, "Here's the gourmet kitchen." If you're selling an insurance policy, describe the security that offers your family. Not only after your death, but while you are alive. Paint a picture of your product in the mind of your prospective buyer. You get the picture.

2. Where is the prospective buyer in his/her buying process?

   Ideally, you want to hear your prospects say, "Yes, we want to buy it, and we want to buy today." But face reality! They could be days, months, or possibly years away from signing a contract. Your mission is to find out where they are in the buying process, what they've already decided, and what they still need to do before they can buy. These items could be totally unrelated to you or your product or service. They might include a school, church, or location of employment issue or even a parent or child issue. As a professional salesperson, it's your job to uncover the real issues.

3. What is the next reasonable step your prospects need to take?

   If you can figure out where they are in the decision-making process and what still has to happen before they can buy, then you may be able to ascertain what would be the next logical step for them to take. Note that I said "for *them* to take." You can guide them, but you cannot decide for them.

4. What can you do to get them to take that step?

    Once you have an idea of what your prospective buyers need to do next, you can more easily figure out what you should do next in your sales process. Do everything with the specific intent of helping your prospective buyers to do something they need to do in their buying process.

Keep these four questions in mind when you greet your next prospects. Every interaction gives you an opportunity to learn more about *their* buying processes and who else needs to be involved in *their* decisions. It could be a parent, child, spouse, school, income, or employment issue—or something simple that's holding up the buying decision. The harsh truth is that without knowing where your prospects are in their buying process—plus what they need to do next and what you need to do to inspire them—the time you spend with them is nothing more than a social visit.

Taking that next step takes guts, but is a profitable and mile marking step that will echo in your career.

FIND OUT WHERE YOUR PROSPECTIVE BUYERS ARE IN THEIR BUYING PROCESS.

"Good management consists in showing average people how to do the work of superior people."

—John D. Rockefeller

Chapter 19

The Marketing Path to Success

Today's complex and fast-changing environment requires you to pay attention to a particularly important segment of sales: marketing.

The marketing process provides a method for management to quickly respond to changing wants and needs of their client base as well as to new products or services, to competition, and to economic conditions. But first I want to dispel the widely held notion that marketing and sales are interchangeable terms or processes. While marketing and sales are certainly related, they function completely differently. As a friend in the auto industry told me, "It's marketing that brings customers into my showroom; its sales that ensures that the customer leaves driving the car." Marketing involves planning, analysis, and projections that, if done correctly, lead to the right product or service at the right price at the right time for a particular buying segment. Make these five steps part of your marketing efforts:

1. Determine your target markets.

    During my seminars and workshops, I ask, "Where is your target market, do you know who they are, do you know where they are? Where are you spending your prospecting time and dollars? Who do you want to attract into your sales office?" Far too often, all I get back are blank stares! Yet most markets are larger than we thought—if for no other reason than a rapidly increasing population. In most cases, we don't market to the vast potential that actually exists.

    Properly identifying and defining your markets, however, requires starting with a systematic *marketing process.* Sales professionals need to know and understand this process if they are to succeed.

2. Analyze opportunities to meet buyers' needs.

    The contribution of the marketing process to the success of a sales organization, especially when sales are down, lies in its commitment to analyze future opportunities to meet customer needs. The marketing process offers a professional planning approach that ends with a detailed plan to sell well-defined products or services to specific market segments.

3. Do budgeting and forecasting.

   Budgeting and forecasting, like sales, will always be necessary for an organization's success. Through both sales forecasts and revenue projections, market planning focuses on identifying what products or services will be sold and to whom. With effective and accurate financial planning in place, both managers and salespeople can make better decisions.

   As a managerial process, creating a marketing plan logically comes out of a series of activities that lead to setting marketing objectives and forming plans for achieving them. Conceptually, you use a planning system designed to identify a range of options for your sales center over a set period.

4. Create a strategic marketing plan.

   The formal marketing process starts by first creating a strategic marketing plan for a three-year (or more) period. It takes the form of a written document from management that outlines the following:

   1. How management perceives its own position in the market relative to its competitors' position

(with competitive advantages and disadvantages accurately defined).

2. What objectives they want to achieve.
3. How they intend to achieve them.
4. What resources are required?
5. What results are expected?

5. Develop a tactical marketing plan from the strategic plan.

A vital segment of a strategic marketing plan is the tactical marketing plan. This details scheduling and costing of specific actions necessary to achieve the first year of the strategic marketing plan. To be effective, the strategic marketing plan *must always* be done before the tactical plan. Unsuccessful companies often rely on sales forecasts and their associated budgets. The problem with this approach is that many salespeople and managers sell to the customers they find easiest to sell to—like people with bad credit. These people eagerly give a deposit, hoping that the salesperson will work a miracle to get their credit approval, but that's not a good long-term approach. By developing and implementing short-term tactical marketing plans first, managers succeed in extrapolating their own shortcomings.

Before you can write a marketing plan and it should always be in writing, set your topics for discussion. I prefer that a well-written marketing plan contain the following:

MISSION STATEMENT: Sets out the mission of the company, covering its role, business definition, competence, and future indications.

FINANCIAL SUMMARY: Summarizes the financial implication over the full planning period.

MARKET OVERVIEW: Provides a brief but important picture of the market, including market trends and key market segments.

COMPETITION ANALYSIS: Analyzes the strengths and weaknesses of your company compared with your competitors.

ISSUES TO BE ADDRESSED: Derived primarily from the competition analysis.

ASSUMPTIONS: Lists the underlying assumptions critical to achieving the planned marketing objectives and strategies.

MARKETING OBJECTIVES: Describes what your company wishes to achieve—usually a quantitative statement in terms of profit, volume, value, and market share over a set time.

MARKETING STRATEGIES: States how objectives are to be achieved and includes the four P's of marketing: product, price, place, and promotions.

RESOURCE REQUIREMENT AND BUDGET: Shows the

full planning period budget along with associated revenues and costs for each year.

Each one is as important as the next. Not one stands out, but when you think positively things will fall into place.

Successful market planning is the cornerstone for developing strong, durable, and robust companies. Given the complexity of a rapidly changing market and the high number of variables that influence business performance, managers require an effective, well-thought-out means of making the situation manageable. The old "shoot from the hip" method of managing has been replaced by a thorough and detailed analysis of how to meet future needs of your particular buying segment.

When done correctly, your marketing plan provides not only a reliable method for building long-term success, but it enables the organization's vision to become a reality. *And that's a big help for those in sales!*

YOUR MARKETING PLAN TURNS YOUR ORGANIZATION'S VISION INTO REALITY.

"An Army of Sheep Lead by a Lion will always defeat an army of Lions led by a Sheep."

—Henry A Thomas

Chapter 20

So, You've Decided to Be a Sales Manager

Law of Averages:

Consider if you will: 1 out of 10 people will walk into a store, let's say a Wal-Mart, Target, Best Buy, or even a Home Depot, and buy something without a salesperson asking them whether they want to buy something or not. Now, let's use our sales prowess to good use:

Wrap your finger around this: statistically 3 out of ten people will buy a product if confronted, or for lack

> of a better term sold on a particular item. Knowledge about the product and relaying that to the consumer is a key factor in that it allows the consumers to think outside the box and discover something new, or put a spin on something old, but also consider this: Allowing the consumer to touch the product as they are perusing. Think about the time you went to buy a drill. Did you want a drill? No, you wanted a hole, but you had to purchase the drill complete with bits, in order to get the size hole you wanted.
>
> Statistically speaking this increases the chances of a consumer buying your product 10 to 20 percent higher. Physical touch is key to get the consumer to "wrap their fingers" around a product. We started with a 10 percent buy value with no one asking about the product. The consumer is just buying, possibly on impulse or window shopping. We drastically improve to 30 percent with knowledge of a particular item and friendly confrontation. Then we have 40–50 percent of consumers buying a product after they have felt it. The mere presence of a salesperson can be intimidating; however, with the right attitude that sales person can be helpful and on a long road to success. The consumer's perception will be one of customer service, instead of a hard sell.

You want to be the best sales manager that you are capable of being. As a first step, *don't panic*! You may initially feel as though you're in over your head. Suddenly a hundred demands are placed on you; you hardly get a chance to catch your breath.

Overnight, you are faced with a mountain of paperwork and people asking you to do something for them. You have a thousand details that demand your immediate attention. Your e-mail in-box is full, and your to-do list seems endless.

To create order out of chaos, consider your objectives and set your priorities. Make a list of the most important issues. Make sure the concepts of maintaining high per-person production, high-employee retention, a highly profitable sales center, and great customer loyalty show up on this initial list. That's what separates the "just okay" sales managers from the great ones. Now, start to manage!

Keep these five principles in mind as you nurture your sales staff:

1. Rehire your best.

> Your best people represent your biggest threat when they leave and your biggest opportunity when they stay or return. Whenever management changes, the risk of losing the best performers increase substantially because having a strong bond between good salespeople and their manager is vital to good performance. As a new manager, you need to re-establish and reinforce this bond as quickly as possible.
>
> Mediocre managers seldom realize the role they play in retaining talent. They assume that people leave because of better offers. They see themselves

as bystanders in a process that they can't control. Unfortunately, these managers simply never develop the strong relationships that help companies hold on to great salespeople.

Great managers, on the other hand, aren't afraid to get close to their best people. They understand that strong relationships enhance productivity.

2. Create and maintain a climate of success.

A sales manager plays a major role in establishing a company's sales culture. Is it upbeat, vibrant, goal-orientated? Is it accomplishment driven? Remember, the title alone doesn't make one a sales manager—leadership does. A good sales manager creates a culture in which star performers thrive. When sales stars decide to work for a company, they also pick a sales manager.

You've probably heard a sports figure state, "I wanted to play for a particular team because of the coach." A sales manager must create that same inviting atmosphere. Highly motivated performers always demand having a manager who brings out the best in them—who can help them achieve their goals. I suggest you respond quickly to the needs of your stars and help them solve their problems.

3. Appreciate uniqueness.

Many managers (particularly new ones) assume that because they were successful with a certain sales style, everyone on their sales team must sell that way. During my sales training, I often hear new managers state, "I thought that is why they promoted me. I was one of the best salespeople in the company. If I could only get everyone to sell the same way I did, they would be just as productive."

That's not a good rule of thumb! Talented, creative people differ from one another, and this is especially true in sales. You don't expect your best salespeople to sell and act the same way; therefore, you shouldn't make the mistake of getting them to imitate your sales style.

Excellence as a manager does not come from getting others to be just like you; it comes from getting others to be more like themselves. Discovering each person's strengths is a secret shared by great managers who use their strengths to develop their talents.

4. Lead from strength.

Average managers believe in the "equality myth," which says that everyone should be treated in the same way. They bend over backward to avoid playing favorites. But great managers view this myth for what it is—politically correct and patently unproductive.

Great managers lead from strength, and that means matching talents with opportunities and resources. Your job is to apportion scarce resources to produce maximum results, not spread them around equally. Although you likely think about the "return on your investment" with money, how do you get the highest returns on your most critical resource—your time?

Helping Weak Players Improve

What produces greater results, spending time with poor performers or spending time with great performers? Too often, new managers believe it's best to spend time with the former. I'm often asked, "How can I help my weak performers improve if I don't spend time with them?" It's easy to fall into this trap, but remember, your job requires you to be a manager/leader, not a professor. Any company's best performers like to have an audience more than an instructor. They want someone who sees and acknowledges their stellar work. Directed in the right way, your presence and encouragement should bring out the best in them. In the same way that athletic teams play better in front of their home crowd, the best salespeople need you to both appreciate them and applaud their results. And it's your job as a sales manager to do just that!

Here are a few guidelines to follow as you strengthen your leadership skills.

1. Aspire to having the qualities of a leader.

   Ponder these leadership challenges to determine how you feel being a leader.

   - If you want to lead, where do you start?
   - Do you think leaders are born or made?

- What leadership skills do you currently possess?
- What leadership skills do you need?
- Are you tired of being a follower?

2. Take these actions to show true leadership.

If you want to be a leader, here is what it takes:

MAINTAIN A POSITIVE ATTITUDE: Be solution-oriented, action-oriented, and people-oriented. Enthusiasm begets success.

EMBRACE CHANGE: Change is certain. Followers tend to resist change. The mark of a leader is to embrace change and take advantage of the opportunity it presents.

DISPLAY COURAGE: General Douglas MacArthur said, "Courage is just fear that holds out a little longer." General George S. Patton said, "I don't take counsel from my fears." True leaders choose and exhibit courage.

TAKE RISKS: The biggest risk is to never take one. Leaders are determined to win. They risk doing new things again and again!

LISTEN: Leaders listen in order to learn. Your salespeople and prospects know their needs, and they know what's happening in their personal and business lives. *Just listen!*

COMMUNICATE: Leaders set an example for open

communication. They use their heads, they say what they feel, and they speak from their hearts.

DELEGATE AND EMPOWER: Leaders share responsibility. They don't dictate; they set examples for others to follow. Leaders encourage growth in others by challenging them to take new responsibilities, encouraging them to succeed, *and supporting them if they fail.* Leaders understand that mistakes are lessons on the way to success.

UNDERSTAND OTHERS, YOURSELF, AND YOUR SITUATION: Leaders understand the importance of an open, inquisitive mind. A constant quest for knowledge brings greater understanding and abilities.

COMMITMENT: Commitment is the catalyst that makes all other leadership qualities a reality. Daily rededication to commitment is the difference between leaders and would-be leaders.

GETTING STARTED: Start small—lead a group or committee. Do whatever it takes to make it a winning experience. Do it again until it begins to feel natural. Respect the power of leadership and the power of the people you seek to lead.

Want to know if certain employees have leadership qualities? A simple, non-costly way is to encourage them to join a charitable organization or a civic club.

If they have true leadership abilities, those members will put themselves in leadership roles. Volunteers will only follow a true leader.

Stop managing and start leading! Sales managers, beware. No one wants just a manager, but everyone wants a leader.

3. Improve the selection process to improve the quality of manager.

Have you ever met poor-performing sales managers who think they're doing a great job? While there are thousands of sales managers (and bosses) who do a superb job, an equal number do not. In defense of the many sales managers who do fail, it's not always their fault. Consider the following all-too- familiar examples.

Many sales managers have risen through the ranks and have a track record of superior sales performance. In recognition of their past sales performances, they are made managers *without any or minimal training* in managing people. Most of these "managers" are now set to fail their company twice: first, because they're unprepared and untrained for the job and, second, because they've left their former position as a sales superstar, thereby creating a void in sales volume.

Remember, managing and leading people require a different set of skills, knowledge, and abilities than what's needed to be a good salesperson. Stated another way, the best tennis player does not necessarily make the best tennis coach.

4. Make sure managers have relevant expertise.

To be effective, good managers require expertise in these seven areas:

1. Administration—Setting policy, dealing with reports, and ensuring that the flow of paper (from orders in to commissions out) is error-free. Must be able to coordinate the selling, delivering, and servicing processes.
2. Recruiting—Able to find and solicit people qualified to sell for the company.
3. Hiring—Can determine by questions, responses, and gut feeling the best candidate for, and most likely to succeed in, a sales position. Once a person is selected, it's necessary to explain all expectations of the job, set sales goals, and get and give commitments to specific performance. *Note*: The best way to do this is to draft a commitment document that specifies what the company will do and what the salesperson will do, including specific sales goals. Then have both parties sign the document and review it at every performance evaluation.

4. Training—If you want both you and your sales team to win, win, win, you'd better train, train, and train. Lead weekly training meetings, have on-the-job staff training, attend sales and man agement seminars, listen daily to sales and man agement tapes, and read at least six books a year on management, sales, and self-improvement.

5. Motivating—To achieve success, create an atmo sphere in which success can occur. This means that a continuous, positive, and supportive atmo sphere helps everyone. So does recognizing and rewarding great performances. If a manager uses his or her power/position to show "who's the boss," three things will happen:

- There will be a high turnover of staff, especially within the sales staff.
- The manager will blame everyone but himself or herself.
- This manager will eventually get fired after causing thousands of dollars worth of damage.

6. Selling—Managers and trainers who don't sell every day lose touch with the realities of a sales-focused environment. How can you lead your sales force if you don't know what your custom ers need? Schedule a regular pattern of selling with the sales staff (in a non-competing way) and speak with every prospective buyer. The

rule behind this is simple: If you aren't selling, you certainly can't lead by example.

7. Lead by Example—This applies to all aspects of the six areas noted. Don't tell someone to do something; show him or her how to do it, and then provide the support, training, resources, and time to get it done. If you want your sales team to succeed, you must be able to lead the way. Stated another way, get your staff to follow you, not your rules.

5. Develop a personal philosophical framework.

It's vital that you spend the time necessary to develop, put into writing, and then follow your own philosophical point of view. Once you do, you'll have a framework within which to operate. You can never be a true leader if you react randomly to each and every situation that comes along. To be a leader, exhibit a high degree of consistency and predictability. And developing your personal philosophy will help you to do just that.

As a guide in developing your personal philosophy of business behavior, you may want to consider my personal do's and don'ts list that has helped me to be a success:

- Control impulsiveness.
- Be aware of blind spots.

- Delegate with confidence (but follow up).
- Consider all options and accept responsibility.
- Never go to war where there are no spoils.
- Be accurately informed. Always get the full story.
- Contemplate the consequences of both your words and your actions, *before you take them.*
- Take calculated risks.
- Be cost-effective with your time.
- Carefully consider what you put in writing. Whatever you write or e-mail, you should feel okay about it appearing on the company bulletin board, printed in a paper of general circulation, read at a meeting of all employees, and/or noted in a court of law. If what you intend to write does not meet these criteria, *do not put it in writing!* Lastly, I strongly suggest you consider one additional point in creating your personal philosophy: Every problem, every disastrous situation, and/or every change has within it an opportunity. And if you look with an open mind, you can *always* find it.

FIND AND FOCUS ON THE OPPORTUNITIES,
NOT ON THE PROBLEMS.

About the Author

Henry Thomas is a keynote speaker, seminar leader, corporate consultant, and as past vice president of a Fortune 200 company, he has been a successful businessman. Henry is a high energy presenter who informs, entertains, and inspires. Both his personal presentations and more than 200 written articles provide critically developed content that offers take home, practical value designed to meet the need of his professional audiences. Henry doesn't just talk business, he lives it every day. He is an entrepreneur with an active interest in many different aspects of business. Above all, he is in touch with the daily challenges confronting the sales profession. Henry shares through experience what works, what doesn't, and what makes the difference. Henry not only shows people what to do but, more importantly, teaches them how to both think and set realistic goals. He is a professional who offers constant excellence, who has a positive outlook on business, and who approaches learning from an integrated perspective.

Henry Thomas is president of henryspeaking, inc.,
a company specializing in sales and leadership training.

Henry can be reached by e-mail at
henry@henryspeaking.com.

www.henryspeaking.com